CO-AYF-138

Jesus

A Sketch of the Man by Theodore P. Ferris

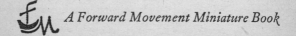
A Forward Movement Miniature Book

FOREWORD

The Story of Jesus as it appears in this book I told first to the congregation of Trinity Church, Boston, on the Sunday mornings in Lent, on Maundy Thursday, Good Friday, Easter, and Whitsunday. I wanted to tell it once again because I found so many adults who had heard it only as children, and were trying to nurture their adult life on food that was prepared for infants. I tried to tell it in such a way as to answer some of the secret questions of their adult minds, and yet not destroy the strong, declarative unfolding of the narrative. I was content to leave out many important details in order to suggest the broad sweep of the story as a whole. I tried to keep my impulse to moralize under reasonable restraint, but from time to time could not resist pointing out a moral consequence or a general observation which the story almost sang out to me.

One cannot help wondering how many times the story has already been told, and how many times it will be told again. And one can only hope that his own telling of it will not be completely unworthy of the story itself, and that those who read it will take at least half as much joy in it as he who told it.

—Theodore P. Ferris

For Frances and Jean Gilmor

CONTENTS

I. THE BIRTH

ONCE AGAIN I venture to tell the story of Jesus. I shall tell it not just as it stands but with enough commentary to make it live, and to relate it to our own lives. And I must say at the beginning that I shall not tell it from an unbiased or unprejudiced point of view. It never has been told from such a point of view, and you must not be surprised if the point of view of the teller is obvious throughout the telling of the story.

No one, I suppose, will be hearing it for the first time; some may be hearing it *virtually* for the first time, hearing it for the first time with their ears really open to it, in a mood that is receptive to it. But, for most of you, it will be the old, old story that you have heard over and over again. Yet in some strange way this particular story never grows old, for it is a story about man and God; about life and death, suffering and sin, joy and sorrow, and, above all, love.

No one, I think, has ever been changed by speculations about Jesus, but people through the centuries have been miraculously changed by Jesus himself. And one of the ways in which men and women these days can meet Jesus is to hear the old story again.

It begins, like most stories about people, with his birth. It begins with sources and origins. Like a stream those sources and origins are difficult to trace. Mists like those that often lie low over the hills where streams have their beginning lie also over the beginnings of this life that began in Galilee. Records were hard to keep in those days, when there were no printing presses; they were not easy to preserve, and even if there had been any bureau of vital statistics, it is likely that the figures would have long since been forgotten. Also, in those days there was much less curiosity about the biographical details of private lives than there is today. We are not surprised, therefore, to find in the story of Jesus' birth fact mingled with legend. Let us look at the facts first.

I

The first fact in the story of Jesus is that he was born. No one seriously doubts that fact; in the nineteenth century, when it was fashionable to doubt everything, there were scholars who raised serious questions about whether Jesus ever lived or not. I think it is safe to say that they have all been answered and that no reputable historian or scholar, whether he be a believer in Christ or not, seriously doubts the fact that Jesus was born and that he lived. It is significant that he was *born;* he did not appear, he did not suddenly descend upon the earth full-blown, full-grown, as Venus is said to have appeared out of the sea. He submitted to the discipline of growth that is implied in the incident of birth, and all the hardships of childhood, if you will, and the agonies of adolescence. His life, like ours, was a gradual unfolding of a personality in all its power and wonder.

When God comes into human life, he does not often take short cuts. He comes by way of the paths he himself has made. And so, when Jesus came into our world, he came by way of birth. That is the first fact.

He was born a Jew. That is the second fact about his life. The Jews were a "proud but unhappy people." They had had practically no success politically, they were not successful militaristically, and they lived most of their lives under the domination of other peoples. They did have, however, an extraordinary flair for religion; they were miles ahead of other people in that one area of life. And to their everlasting credit stands the fact that they were the first to discover that the physical powers from which the universe is derived and the moral forces in life are the same. They realized that God was the source not only of power but of moral law, and so they made that marriage between religion and ethics for which all the world owes them a debt. One of the tragic things that may be said about the history of the Western World is that we are likely to remember the Jews as the people who killed Jesus. We might better remember the Jews as the people who produced Jesus.

Another fact in the story of his birth is that he was born of humble parents. In the religion of the Jews in those days it was appropriate to offer sacrifices to God—live, animal sacrifices. A pigeon was a poor man's sacrifice, and when Joseph and Mary came to present Jesus to the temple and to offer the sacrifice that was appropriate at that time, they offered a pair of pigeons, the implication being that they were too poor to afford anything more costly. Joseph was most certainly a carpenter by trade, but he was a carpenter with royal blood in his veins; he could trace his ancestry back to David. How much that means, we are not altogether certain. Just about the same number of years elapsed between Jesus and David as between us and William the Conqueror, and it is very likely that there are many people in the British Isles who can show that they are descended from William the Conqueror without its making very much difference in their lives. But the fact remains that these parents of humble circumstances had the royal blood of David running in their veins, and the memory of better days.

What about the time and the place of the birth? Those are two facts that are of great interest to modern men and women. The place is fairly certain—Bethlehem—although there are discrepancies in the two stories of the birth, one in Matthew and one in Luke, which have made some people wonder if Jesus was born in Bethlehem or not. You probably remember that according to Matthew, Joseph and his family lived in Bethlehem, so naturally Jesus was born there, at home, and the family went to Nazareth only because they wanted to avoid persecution. In Luke's story, however, they lived in Nazareth, and they went to Bethlehem in order to comply with the rules of the Roman government and to register there for the census. I think most people, however, are agreed that it is safe to accept as fact that Jesus was born in Bethlehem, the city of David.

The date is not quite so certain; scholars put it about four years before the beginning of our era, calculating by the known dates of the rulers under whom the events described transpired. The significant thing about the date of Jesus' birth, however, is not so much the year he was born as it is something else. We all determine the date of our birth by the calendar. In the case of Jesus alone, the date of his birth determines the calendar. It was that fact that inspired the great English philosopher, Alfred North Whitehead, to make this comment: "The life of Christ has the decisiveness of a supreme ideal, and that is why the history of the world divides at this point of time." So much for the facts.

II

Now let us look at the legends. We are always a little frightened by the word legend, especially when it is used in reference to anything that is religious. Somehow we think that a legend is something not true, so that when anything is labeled a legend we are apt to discredit it, and set it aside as slightly suspicious. As a matter of fact, there is always a kernel of fact at the heart of every legend. Every legend begins with a fragment of history. And a legend about a person can often tell us more about what he was like than volumes of documented history. So don't be afraid of legends. They are the attempt of men and women to say in story what they have come to believe about a person; they are a tribute that men and women humbly offer to the people they most adore.

There is a cluster of legends that have gathered around the birth of Jesus. There is a wonderful legend that his mother knew even before he was born that he was destined to be a king, and that she knew this not merely by a mother's intuition or instinct, but by a message straight from God, delivered by none other than the Angel Gabriel himself. There is a legend that Jesus was born in a stable, as if people wanted to say right at the beginning that he was rejected from the start, that somehow or other there never was room for him in the world, even at the moment of birth, when normally the whole world opens its heart and its doors to take in a mother and her baby.

There is the legend that the angels sang when he was born, and a bright star appeared in the sky, as if people wanted to say, "This is a momentous fact; this is something that concerns more than a little village in Palestine—the repercussions of it echo from the very skies themselves." There is the legend that shepherds came to see him, as though people wanted to make clear that it was the plain people who responded to him first, and with gladness. And then astrologers came from the east, giving him the richest gifts they could find, as though men were trying to say that the leaders of thought who were popular in that day recognized the fact that their day was done, their sun set, and that from henceforth the center of life and thought, as far as human beings were concerned, was none other than this baby born in Bethlehem.

And then there is the legend that Herod tried to get rid of Jesus by killing all the other babies in the region, as though men saw from the very beginning that his claim to royalty was somehow implicit in him even as a child, that his simple goodness was a threat to every throne and crown. And finally, there is the legend that appeals to all parents: how Joseph and his family fled into Egypt to escape the persecution and save the precious child. So the legends have grown up around the birth of Jesus, fragments of fact wreathed with garlands of adoring tributes.

You remember that the small log cabin in Kentucky in which Abraham Lincoln was born has been enclosed in a massive Greek temple. People realized, you see, that there was a massiveness about the life of Lincoln that the simple log cabin might not indicate to the untrained eye. And so as a sort of sad, almost pitiful, yet at the same time powerful sign of the fact that they did not completely miss the massiveness of that life, they built a massive Greek temple to crown the log cabin. So in sincerity, sometimes misguided, sometimes misplaced, men have added to the birth of Jesus the legends that seem to them true, to indicate that here was something momentous that a stable in Bethlehem might not make clear to the untrained eye.

III

The question about the Virgin Birth remains. Is it fact or legend? Christians do not all agree. The majority accept the statements in Matthew and Luke, that Jesus was born not of a human father but conceived by the Spirit of God. The majority of Christians, I think it is fair to say, accept that statement as fact. Others are inclined to accept the silence of Mark and John and Paul and every other writer of the New Testament—plus many other considerations that we cannot go into now—as pointing toward legend. It is only fair for me to say here that I myself belong to this latter group. In whichever group you find yourself, it is

13

dangerous and unwise to be dogmatic about it. The important thing is this: whether the story of the Virgin Birth be fact or legend, the meaning is the same, *that Jesus came from God*.

We all come from God; our very lives are derived from a power not of ourselves. If it were not for God, we should not be alive. But Jesus comes from God more directly, with a more specific intention; he comes to do what only God can do, namely to show us himself and to save us from ourselves. People felt that from the beginning, at first perhaps vaguely, but, as time went on, with increasing clarity. Here is one of the sons of men, they said, who is the Son of God. He comes from God to show us God, and to save us from our sins. And in addition to saying that Jesus comes from God, Christians began to see that God came in Jesus, and that in this human being there is a strange, mysterious commingling of the divine and the human not to be found elsewhere, so that in him we see the Father, and through him we find life, forgiveness, reassurance, and renewal, re-establishment in the family of God.

Now the only way that the ordinary minds of unimaginative men and women can take that in is in narrative form. (The Jews always cast their doctrine in the form of a story.) If Jesus comes from God, then he must be the Son of God, and if he is the Son of God, then of course God is his father and he cannot have a human father such as Joseph. If you have a mind like that, take that narrative as the best description of something that is everlasting true. If you do not have a mind like that, take the narrative as a sign and an indication, from people who have lived close to Christ, that he comes from God, and that God comes in him. That is the important thing to remember about his birth; not just that he was another person entering into this difficult arena of life to be snuffed out in his early thirties, but that he was a gift from God, in whom there is life and light and love for us now and for all eternity.

That is the story of Jesus' birth and it is the story that rings down through the ages and is as alive now as it ever was. No wonder when one man read it he wrote this:

> *I know not how that Bethlehem's babe*
> *Could in the Godhead be;*
> *I only know the manger child*
> *Has brought God's life to me.*

* Reprinted by permission of the Hymn Society of America.

II. THE BAPTISM

THE STORY of Jesus jumps from his birth to his baptism almost thirty years later. There is only one brief reference to those intervening years. Luke tells us that when Jesus was twelve years old his parents took him to Jerusalem for one of the great religious holidays. He found himself so much at home in the temple, and became so interested in what the teachers in the temple had to say, that he forgot all about his parents and was left behind by mistake. The rest is silence.

That silence has tempted people to speculate. Some have fancied that during those eighteen years (between the visit to the temple and his baptism) Jesus traveled in Egypt and India, and there became well acquainted with the religion and philosophy of those mystic lands. Other people have been so bold as to speculate that during those years he experienced love, marriage, and parenthood. And even so dependable a student as John Erskine in his book *The Human Life of Jesus* concluded that because Jesus understood women so well and loved children so much he must have had a more intimate knowledge of them than would have been possible in his public ministry.

Such speculation is idle at its best, and dangerous at its worst. Those years have been called "the hidden years." It is, in my judgment at least, best not to pry behind the curtain that hides them from our curious gaze. We know this much: we know that Jesus was brought up in the little town of Nazareth, and was therefore subject to all the influences of a small town. We know that he was the eldest of five sons and the brother of at least two sisters. We know that his father was a carpenter and that he probably learned his father's trade and practiced it, and that in the year 150 there was a man who said that he had seen the plows and the yokes that Jesus the carpenter had made. And we know, too, that when he was about thirty, or probably a little younger, he left Nazareth, his family and his trade and his friends, his home and all his responsibilities, and that he never went back, except for a brief visit. Now, why did Jesus leave Nazareth?

I

Perhaps he wanted to get away from home—not because his home was not a good home, for there is every indication that it was, and not because he was not a good son, for we have every reason to believe that he was—but because he was a normal young man and it is the natural desire of most young people, sooner or later, to leave the nest, to see the world, to live their own lives, to stand on their own feet, to try their own wings, to stretch their own limbs, and to broaden their own horizons. And so, in every generation the towers of the distant city have glittered in the sunlight and attracted the eyes of the earnest youth up in the hills, and he has not been able to rest until he has turned his steps thitherward to pursue those glistening towers in the distance. The tragedy of many a young life is that it has never peered over the walls of its own back yard.

A more obvious reason, and one perhaps nearer the truth, is that Jesus wanted to see a contemporary of his called John. Tradition has it that these two young men, about the same age, were cousins. They lived far apart and apparently never saw much of each other, except at this one period of their lives. Whether they were kin by blood or not, we do not know; we do know that they had several things in common. Both had intensely religious natures; they were deeply concerned about the things of God. Their spirits were attuned to invisible, intangible things; and both were concerned with the moral failure of their own people, the Jews. They were both direct descendants of the prophets. And when they analyzed the situation they saw all around them, the situation of distress and disaster and internal decay, they were likely to put most of the blame not on their enemies and not on the external influences of their environment, but upon their own failure to respond to the will of God. And both were convinced that something was going to happen soon, that they were on the threshold, on the verge, of a new era. For John it was a dark day of judgment, and for Jesus it was a day of new and wonderful life.

At this point, John had gone considerably farther than Jesus—that is, in his active ministry. At the time Jesus left Nazareth, John was already holding open-air meetings in the wild country east of the Jordan. He lived there; he was an ascetic, not only by nature but also by discipline; he ate the simplest food; he dressed as simply as he could; he scorned luxury and the plush existence of the people in Jerusalem, and in order to show his scorn, he lived in the waste places of the wilderness. He held his open-air meetings there, and as he preached, crowds came from Jerusalem and from every corner of Judea.

We should probably call him a revivalist; what he preached was what we should call hell-fire and damnation; he preached a stern message of doom and destruction; he set before the people their moral failures, and he told them, in words that were as vivid as any man could make them, that a day of reckoning was coming in which they would be accounted guilty and, unless they had a change of heart, would be destroyed. He compared them, if you can imagine it, to the snakes that slither away out of the burning stubble when the farmers clean the fields by burning them in the autumn after the harvest.

John not only preached; he baptized people in the river Jordan. People ought to be washed, they needed to be cleansed, according to John. And as they submerged themselves in the dirty waters of the Jordan, they acted in a symbolic way, as though to say that they recognized their sin and their corruption and their mistakes, and were determined to do better in the future. So there was John in the wasteland east of the Jordan, preaching to crowds of people and baptizing them. John was the best there was up to that time, and Jesus left Nazareth and came to see what he was doing. And when he came, and saw, and heard, he went to John and was baptized, like all the rest, in the Jordan.

That may raise the question in your mind, was Jesus then a sinner? John's baptism was explicitly for sinners as a sign of repentance, and a symbol of forgiveness. When Jesus consented to be baptized, did it mean that he admitted that he, too, was a sinner and needed to be washed in the waters of new life? Early Christians were explicit in what they believed. They said, No, a thousand times no. He knew no sin—and the Church has preached the dogma of the sinlessness of Jesus ever since. We in our time may not be quite so sure. We are sure, certainly, that sin had no dominion over him, just as death had no dominion over him. But we may believe that just as Jesus had to cope with temptation, he had to struggle with the consciousness of sin just as you and I do, and that while he came to that point in his mature life where he was master of sin as he was master of his body, there were those earlier days when the mastery was not quite so certain, and when he had to struggle against all those forces that threaten to hold a man down. Personally speaking, the moral mastery of Jesus means more to me if he achieved it than if he was given it at the start.

So, why did Jesus leave Nazareth? There is a still deeper reason. He wanted to be involved in the life of his people and the life of his times. He knew that he *was* involved in the life of his people and the life of his times, and he knew in a sense, I believe, that he was involved even in their sin, socially if not personally. And so he identified himself with the people; he did not hold himself aloof; he went down into the muddy, dirty waters of the Jordan just as all the rest of the people did. He accepted the sign of John's baptism, which was at that point the best there was. He threw his weight on the side of the strongest religious influence of his day.

The record reads quite simply: "And it came to pass in those days that Jesus came from Nazareth of Galilee, and was baptized by John in the Jordan." What happened when Jesus was baptized?

II

The record tells us—that is, the record according to St. Mark—that as Jesus came up out of the waters he saw the heavens opened. Apparently nobody else saw anything or heard anything unusual. It was a subjective, religious experience that Jesus went through. Before, in his earlier life, those first twenty-nine or thirty years, there had been intimations that he was meant for something special in life, that God had sent him into this world to perform some specific task of unique significance. There had been glimpses and glances and guesses; there had been brief interludes of certainty, and then periods of obscurity and uncertainty. But now, as he came up out of the waters of the Jordan, the heavens, says Mark, *split*. It is a verb that suggests violence; they were torn asunder, literally rent in twain. Most of us have had the experience of seeing clouds that are black as night, and are so ominous that we can hardly dare to believe that the sun is behind them, suddenly split in two by the piercing rays of the sun.

Before it was uncertainty. Now as he comes out of the

water there is clarity and certainty, truth and illumination. He knows what God wants him to do. And when he later described the experience to his friends, he put it in specific, visual language, as we should expect. He said it was as though the spirit of God, like a dove, descended upon him; as though something from above, greater than himself, came down upon him and took possession of him; as though from thenceforward a power filled him that was a power greater than himself, giving him strength and energy to withstand all difficulties. It was the power like the power of a dove —suggesting that early picture of the creation, in which the spirit of God, like a great bird, brooded over the chaos of the universe, and by his brooding made order out of that chaos. So, Jesus said, in that moment it was as though the heavens opened and the spirit like a dove came down and took possession of him, and from that time on the way was clear.

And he went on to say that he heard a voice, and the voice said to him, "Thou art my son, in whom I am well pleased." It was the voice speaking in the words of a psalm Jesus had heard all his life; it was the Second Psalm, which was used for the coronation of a king. That says more than anything we can say by way of commentary. What Jesus was trying to say was something like this: as he saw the heavens open and the spirit of God descend upon him, he was conscious of the fact that God had chosen him: "You are the one," the voice said, "you are the one to show my people my way, you are the one to reveal my love to them, you are the one I have chosen; your way will not be easy and your destiny is hard and difficult, but you are the one."

So Jesus came up out of the waters of the Jordan with

a vision of God's purpose and his own destiny, and that vision was to sustain him through all the unfair opposition in Galilee, through the disloyalty of his friends, through the darkness of Gethsemane, through the unjust trial in Jerusalem, and finally through the blackness of Calvary.

I should like to make three comments on this vision as we think of it in terms of our own lives. *Every life that amounts to anything begins with a vision,* the vision of something that commends itself as supremely desirable and ultimately valuable. The vision may not come until the person is seventy years old; in that case, life does not begin until seventy. Every life that amounts to anything begins with a vision. To take this out of the realm of specifically religious life, think of Agnes DeMille. All of us who appreciate the ballet and the modern theater know what Agnes DeMille has done for it and how much delight she has given us with her American ballets. In the story of her life she tells us that from the time she was thirteen she knew that she wanted to be a dancer. As is often the case, her family did not give her much encouragement, and she went through those early years wondering if she could ever accomplish her purpose. And then, when she was thirteen, she saw Pavlova dance. This is what she says: "Before our dazzled eyes she flashed with the sudden sweetness of a humming bird in action too quick for our understanding. I sat with the blood beating in my throat. As I walked into the afternoon my head ached and I could scarcely swallow. I didn't wish to cry, I certainly couldn't speak." For that young girl, Agnes DeMille, on that day the heavens opened, and her life began at that moment, with a vision.

The second comment is this. The visions of life always lead to decisions, and Agnes DeMille can take us into this second step of our journey, for she writes the following about the evening of the same day: "As I climbed the stairs slowly to my bedroom and, shutting myself in, placed both hands on the brass rail at the foot of my bed, then rising laboriously to the tips of my white-buttoned shoes I stumped the width of the bed and back again." There was the decision, and there was the beginning of the discipline that makes a dancer. And so, as we follow the way of Jesus, we must be prepared to follow him into the valley of decision, for his vision, like everybody's vision, led him into the valley where great decisions had to be made and grave disciplines undertaken. We shall follow him into that valley.

The third comment is this—and the comments become more solemn and more grave. The vision comes, I think, to those who are not afraid of the muddy waters of the Jordan. As Jesus came up out of the water, the heavens opened. It seems to me, as I observe my contemporaries and try to understand myself, that one of the fears most likely to paralyze our life is our fear of becoming involved in anything, the fear of getting tied up with something that might mean losing some of our freedoms. I know wonderful people in middle life who are afraid of becoming involved in marriage and a family; they do not want to lose their freedom. Other people are afraid of becoming involved in the corruption of the world, and so they stay in a little private backwater somewhere, where nothing can interfere with their personal lives. There are others who are so afraid of becoming involved in anything, or of being committed to a life that means anything, that they live in virtual isolation and have no visions—because they never are willing to go down into the dirty waters of the Jordan.

As we come to the end of this story of the vision of Jesus, you may say, "But I have no visions; my life goes on rather monotonously and without much interest; I am past middle age, my mountain peaks are behind me; and I go about my job and try to do it as well as I can, but there is no excitement in me. I don't look for any new visions." Or you may be young, and as you look forward to your uncertain future your attitude is the same: "I have never had any great visions; there is nothing that I want to do particularly in life; nothing has ever stirred those depths in me that you talk about in the lives of other people."

Of course, no one person, certainly not a preacher, can adequately answer that question and speak to that situation. All I should like to say is this, which may point the way. Remember Stephen, one of the youngest, boldest, earliest followers of Jesus. He paid a price for following Jesus (because Christians were feared then and were unpopular) and they put him to death. And as they stoned him, Stephen looked up and said, "Behold, I see the heavens opened, and the Son of man standing on the right hand of God." It was Jesus whom he saw, and as he was dying he said, "Lord Jesus, receive my spirit." And then rising to an even greater height, drawn up by the greatness of the vision that he saw, he said, "Lord, lay not this sin to their charge." He for whom the heavens once opened, when he came up out of the waters, is himself the opening of heaven for us. He is our vision, and he is now choosing you and me, and he is speaking to us, and what he says is this: "You are the one I choose to live a life of forgiving, understanding love like mine. I choose you. That is your task, that will be your crown."

III.   THE
         TEMPTATION

So FAR we have followed the story of Jesus from his birth
through his baptism. When Jesus came up out of the waters
of the Jordan in which he had been baptized by John, the
heavens opened; there was a moment of clear vision, of
exaltation and exhilaration. His mission in life at that time
was made indubitably clear; he was to be the one to save
his people.

Now we come to the more somber story of the temptation. "And Jesus was led by the spirit into the wilderness,
being forty days tempted of the devil." Jesus went from the
high place of vision into the valley of decision.

I

We who have been born and raised in this period of intense interest in science and history thirst for historical
accuracy. We like to know the facts, and the first question
that we are likely to ask about any past event is, What
actually happened? There are, as you know, impressionistic

27

paintings of things that took place in the past, in which the details are submerged in the total meaning of the picture. And then, on the other hand, there are line drawings, in which the details are finely and sharply etched. Most of us, I think, prefer the line drawings. We want to know what happened and what the facts are.

For instance, in this case we want to know how long Jesus was in the wilderness. The record says he was there forty days. Why forty days? Forty, in Jewish literature and in the Jewish way of speaking, is a round number. You remember that Moses was on the mountain fasting in the presence of God for *forty* days. The Israelites were tried and tested in the wilderness for *forty* years. And the length of time from Easter, when Christ rose from the dead, to the day on which he ascended into heaven is *forty* days. It is a round number. When the record says that Jesus was in the wilderness forty days, it means something like this: Jesus was in the wilderness quite a while, several weeks, five or six at least.

We want to know also how he could go that long without food, and if he actually did. It is interesting, as we try to make these historical investigations, to notice that Mark in his account does not say anything about fasting. He never mentions the fact that Jesus went without food while he was in the wilderness. That implies to some of us that the fasting in the story is incidental to the other things that happened. The implication is that Jesus had too many important things on his mind to give much thought or much time to the consideration of food. You remember when Handel wrote *The Messiah,* he did it in two weeks; he locked himself up in his room, and when his faithful valet set his meals outside the door, he touched hardly anything. In some such way, food was not on the mind of Jesus during this long period of testing.

Also, we want to know more about the devil. The story says that Jesus was tempted of the devil, more personally known as Satan. Did Jesus really believe in him? Did Jesus really believe in a personal devil? All the indications are, I think, that he did. Certainly, in the popular literature of the day and in the religion of the time, the devil was the ring leader of the forces of evil. He was a well-known figure; the Jews of that time were in the habit of personifying impersonal forces; they were more dramatic in their way of thinking than we are, and while our psychological imagery may be different from theirs, I am not sure that we have made much improvement, and I think we need not look back upon the people who believed in a personal devil as naïve and uncouth. Did Jesus really see him? Was this encounter that took place an encounter between two visible figures? Almost certainly not. There was no conversation that could be heard; there was no transportation of Jesus from the wilderness to the tower of the temple, or to the mountain top, that could be seen. This struggle was an internal affair, something that went on in the heart and the mind and the spirit of a man. If you had been there, in the same place and at the same time, you might not have been aware of it at all.

We read the story through the eyes of our own experience, and we are bound to do that. Every generation reads the story of Jesus through its own eyes, and to a certain extent colors it by its own experience. There is no way to get away from it. Our eyes are eyes that are psychologically conditioned, and we are bound to read this story through the conditioning of our eyes. We know that periods of ecstasy and exhilaration are likely to be followed by periods of depression. The high spots of life are likely to be followed by low spots, and some are lower than others. And so we are prepared for what happened to Jesus after he had seen the heavens opened and had experienced that moment of clarity and illumination. We are not surprised that he was driven into the wilderness; the wilderness, think of it—unpopulated, uncultivated, unfamiliar, unproductive wasteland; the very picture and imagery of depression and of those low moments in life when we wonder what life is all about.

We know also in a more positive way that visions always lead a man into the valley of decision. We said in the last chapter that at the time of his baptism the mission of Jesus was made clear to him; he was convinced that God had chosen him to save his people. Now the question arose, Save them, how? Save them from what? You see, this vision of his was something that had to be thought through; here great soul searching was demanded, and he went into the wilderness to be tested, to think, to bring all the experience of his early years into focus upon this mighty task and come out of it with the decision about what kind of saviour he intended to be.

II

According to Matthew and Luke, there were three temptations. The first was the temptation to turn stones into bread.

There were more stones in Palestine than anywhere else in the world; they resembled loaves of bread in appearance; no wonder Jesus thought of bread. He was hungry. In this mood of inner searching and depression and downcast spirits, he had neglected food and now he was hungry, and he looked at the stones and thought he might make them into bread. Moreover, he knew that there were thousands of people in his country who were hungry; they had to pay such heavy taxes that they could not afford the necessities of life; they were poor. Jesus wanted to do something to help them. He was the kind of person who was filled with compassion for the ordinary man who did not have enough to buy bread for his table. He wanted to do it. He thought he could do it. If he were the person God said he was, he could do it. Should he do it? Should he use his power and turn these stones into loaves of bread to feed himself and thousands of hungry people in Jewry?

He decided against it. There is something more important in life than food. Jesus apparently came to the conclusion that the welfare state will never save the world. We must make a statement of caution here, for Jesus appreciated the importance of material things, and he told us to give people who are hungry the food they need and the drink they thirst for, but he had a deeper perception. He was more interested in a quality of life than in a standard of living, and when he had to decide whether he wanted to be the economic saviour of the world, or the saviour of men's inner lives and character, he decided in favor of the latter. It is true that a man cannot pray on an empty stomach, but it is also true that many a man with a gloriously full stomach never prays.

Most men are desperate when they are hungry, and they might be tempted to do anything for a loaf of bread. Here, praise God, was one who was not desperate. In spite of his own hunger and the hunger of the people he loved, he was able to look at the situation calmly and coolly in the light of the eternal objectives that he set before himself as the saviour of the world, and in answer to the temptation that came to him in the personified form of Satan, he said, "Man shall not live by bread alone."

The second temptation was the temptation to play for political power. Jesus, from everything we know about him, was shrewd. He was a quick-witted man, his intelligence was sharp. He knew, for instance, that a man could not get very far in the world, and could not influence people, unless he had power. He knew also that most people want to be ruled. And he knew also that you cannot do much with people unless you do rule them. And so, when, in the figurative language of the Gospel, Satan took him up to a high mountain and showed him all the kingdoms of the world over which he might be the ruler, and into which he then might bring the reforms that he so much wanted to bring into the lives of the people, he was strongly tempted to play for political power in order to bring to pass what he wanted to bring to pass. But, fortunately, Jesus also knew that you cannot have political power without compromise, without concessions here and there to people who help your cause, even though they are not the kind of people you would like them to be; without accommodations here and there to the feelings of this one and to the needs and requests of that one; without graft and compensations for this and that person. He knew that there were always people to be paid off. He knew that if he was to have that kind of political power he would lose forever his spiritual power over the lives of men. He knew that he could not play for political power and, at the same time, love his neighbors, to say nothing of his enemies.

Most leaders, both political and spiritual, have made compromises from time to time. They have cut corners, they have taken short cuts, they have made little concessions here and there. Here, praise God, is one who made none. When he was tempted to make compromises in order to rule the nations of the earth, he said, "Thou shalt worship the Lord thy God, and him only shalt thou serve."

The third of the three temptations, and I suspect the most enticing of all, was the temptation to jump off the tower of the temple. People, you know, were no different then than they are now; they crave the spectacular. People are always stimulated by the sensational. And the question in Jesus' mind must have been something like this: if he could get the attention of the people by spectacularly jumping off the temple tower, and being rescued in a miraculous way by God, why not do it? We do not know what went through his mind, but perhaps something like this. "I shall not do it because spectacles go only skin deep." A man who sits on top of a flag pole for three weeks creates a spectacle, and a crowd gathers around him, but when the spectacle is over, what is there left? Jesus may also have thought this as he faced that question: "Man has no right to force God's hand: God has put him in his universe, he has made its laws, he has given him his work to do, and he has no right to try to force his hand by expecting of him the unusual and the miraculous and the spectacular."

Most of the leaders of the world have at one time or another yielded to the temptation to do stunts to capture people's attention, and the leaders of the church are no less susceptible to this temptation than anybody else. One of the easiest things for a minister of the church to do, especially a preacher, is to perform a stunt to capture the attention of the people. Most of the leaders of the world, both political and spiritual, have yielded at one time or another to that temptation. Jesus absolutely refused to do stunts to attract people to himself. And his answer to the Satan who was so real to him in this particular struggle was, "Thou shalt not tempt the Lord thy God."

III

As I have done in the other chapters of the story, I should like to make three brief observations on the temptations. The first is this: all three temptations, you notice, were temptations to do something good, but not good enough. They were not temptations to do something bad. The first was the temptation to feed people; that certainly was a good thing. The second was the temptation to rule people; that certainly can be a good thing. And the third temptation was to give people a sign, and that need not be a bad thing. Now, they were all temptations to do something good, but not good enough. The question that Jesus had to face in himself was, "Shall I do things that are all right in themselves, but which are not the best I know, or shall I continue along lines that I know to be the way of God, even though they do not meet with popular success?"

The greatest temptation for us in life is not to do something bad but to fail to be our best.

And the second observation is this: the subtlest temptation of all in the story, at least as I read and understand it, is only implied, and it is to be found in the phrase that introduces two of the temptations. "If thou be the son of God," make these stones bread. "If thou be the son of God." He had been so sure that he was; he had had intimations all through his early life, and then when he was baptized the heavens opened and he was certain that this mission was his, and that he was in some unique relationship to God, and that this was his task in life. But was he? There came to him again that terrible, haunting thought, "Can I be sure? Maybe I am not. Perhaps this is an illusion of grandeur. Maybe I am a freak. Maybe I am a megalomaniac who thinks that he is the son of God." One of the great temptations in life is to doubt ourselves. There are times when we are sure that we are children of God and inheritors of the kingdom of heaven, and then times get difficult and our whole existence becomes troubled and perplexed by various things that happen to us and we begin to say to ourselves, "I wonder if I really am. Maybe I am just the victim of an illusion; maybe I am not the child of God at all; maybe all these things that I have imagined belonged to me as a child of God are not mine at all." That is one of the great temptations people have—to doubt themselves, who they are, what they are. And for those of us who have chosen what we like to call a vocation—the ministry, teaching, nursing, the medical profession, the law, any of the activities by which we serve our fellow men —there are times in our youth when we are sure that this is the one thing we are meant to do, and then our darkest moment comes, when the question makes its way into our minds, "Maybe I am not what I thought I was." Jesus faced that most subtle of all temptations.

And the third observation is this. The devil finally departed from him, but only for a season, the implication being that these questions kept coming back to Jesus all through life. These same temptations recurred—to work miracles for immediate needs, to play for political power, to give the people a sign and so win popularity for himself. Life's moral struggles are never finished; we never get to the place where we can say, "Well, I've conquered that temptation forever, I'll never be enticed in that direction again." Don't ever think it. For the temptations that bother us and the ones that are really alluring and enticing come again and again, and while there may be periods when the devil, so to speak, departs from us, he departs only for a season and we had best be prepared for his return.

But in the case of Jesus, the decisive battle had been fought and won. Jesus came through this valley of decision with three definite conclusions: No tricks. No stunts. No compromises. And once that decision had been made, what a relief there must have been, a relief of which Mark alone of the evangelists gives us any indication, when he writes in one unforgettable sentence, "And he was with the wild beasts, and angels ministered unto him."

IV. THE MINISTRY

AFTER THE temptation, Jesus went back to Galilee and began his public career.

There are three facts about the public career of Jesus that are worth keeping in the back of your mind as you begin to examine it more closely. First, it covered very little ground. The public life of Jesus was almost completely confined to the little province of Galilee. Except for occasional trips to Jerusalem and visits to the coastal towns of Tyre and Sidon, he rarely left Galilee. Galilee is a province in the northern part of Palestine; it is exactly sixty miles from north to south, and thirty miles from east to west. It is a small place; at that time it was thickly populated, had rich fertile ground, but was unimportant in the affairs of the world. As we think of careers in these days, covering a whole hemisphere if not the world itself, one confined to a little country sixty by thirty miles is an extraordinary thing.

The second fact is that the public career of Jesus lasted a very short time. According to the tradition, it lasted three years. That tradition is based upon the simple fact that in John's Gospel the Passover occurs three times, and the assumption is that Jesus celebrated three successive Passovers in Jerusalem and therefore his public life lasted three years. In recent times we have come to count not quite so much on John's Gospel for historical accuracy and chronology, and in the other three Gospels there is only one Passover. Therefore the conclusion of most people who read the Gospel carefully is that the ministry of Jesus lasted, more likely, about eighteen months, perhaps not much more than a year.

The third fact worth remembering is that when it ended, as it did end, tragically, when Jesus came to Jerusalem and got into trouble with the authorities, it had ostensibly accomplished next to nothing. No organization had been established; no institution was prepared to support it; a few artisans and fishermen had been trained, but they had scattered when the emergency finally arose; there were no written documents of any kind to preserve the words that Jesus had said, and this brief, confined public career of Jesus ended with apparently nothing accomplished.

The question, of course, is how a public career lasting little more than a year, in a country less than half the size of Massachusetts, with no tangible results at the end, could make such a deep and lasting impression upon the history of the human race. I know of no simple answer to that question, but in working toward an answer let us look at a typical day in the public career of Jesus.

I

This particular day was spent in a town called Capernaum. It was a prosperous town on the northern shore of the

Sea of Galilee. Jesus had no permanent station; he had no regular pulpit from which he spoke Sunday after Sunday. He traveled about from place to place, from village to village. He was not even like John, who settled himself in the wilderness and let the people come to him. Jesus did not wait for the people to come to him; he went to the people.

On this day in Capernaum, he had with him four young friends, two pairs of brothers, Simon and Andrew, and James and John. They were the ones he had chosen to travel about with him. He never went anywhere alone, as far as we can see, except to the hills to pray. He always had with him a small group of companions whom he knew rather more intimately than he knew the rank and file of the people; later on he expanded that group to at least twelve, perhaps even more. But at the beginning when this particular day is recorded, there were only four, and we can picture the five young men arriving in the town of Capernaum.

We say to ourselves in passing, as we make our own private commentaries on the story of Jesus, that no movement in life, whether it is a world-wide movement or a movement in our own family, is ever launched by one person alone. It is always done in company with those who understand and are loyal. A leader alone, by himself, is not enough.

On Saturday, the Jewish day of rest and worship, Jesus went to the synagogue. The synagogue, you remember, was an organization carried on almost entirely by laymen, and on this occasion Jesus was invited to preach. It often happened that laymen who had a particular interest in religion were invited to preach when they visited a synagogue away from home.

Jesus talked wherever he went; the story makes that perfectly clear. "Jesus came preaching." He had a way with words, he knew how to tell a story so that no one could ever forget it. He had a kind of directness about his speech that makes it unlike any other speech in the world. The words of Jesus are words that you could never miss. They are characterized by a certain extravagance. "A rich man has as much chance," he said, "to get into the kingdom as a camel has to go through the eye of a needle." "If you have faith like a tiny mustard seed, you can move mountains." His speech was dramatic, vivid, extravagant. He made people remember what he said. He could put volumes in a nutshell: "He that exalteth himself shall be abased, and he that humbleth himself shall be exalted." So, wherever he went on these tours of the villages and towns, he always talked and people always wanted to listen.

What did he talk about? On this particular occasion there is no record of exactly what he said. We know, however, that he invariably talked, wherever he went, about a *Kingdom*. Everybody knew what a kingdom was; they all lived in a kingdom, the biggest and most powerful kingdom that the world had ever known; they lived under the most powerful ruler that the world had ever seen, Tiberius Caesar. So that the minute he began to talk about a kingdom, he was talking about something that everybody understood. But his Kingdom was different. The king of his Kingdom was God, the maker of heaven and earth.

If we wanted to put in one sentence—which is dangerous

as well as difficult—what made Jesus' teaching and talk different from everybody else's, it might be this: Jesus took the rule of God seriously. All the Jews believed in the rule of God; they were taught as children to sing, "The Lord is king, be the people never so impatient." But they did not take it very seriously; they thought that that rule was a long way off and did not have much to do with them, and that they need not pay much attention to it. Once in a while, perhaps, they would sing about it in the synagogue. But the rule of God did not have very much to do with their lives.

Jesus came into their towns and began to talk about the Kingdom of God. He took it seriously. And the key to the Kingdom, as he talked to them about it, was love, unrestrained good will. The standards of God's rule were unbelievably high, no less than perfection; but you were admitted to the Kingdom not on the basis of achievement but on the basis of your attitude of mind. If you could, like a child, trust God and accept his rule, then God would give you the Kingdom. The Kingdom was not something you had to build or make; the Kingdom was life that God was ready to give you.

As Jesus talked about it, he tried to make men see things this way: if you really accept God's rule in your life, that is the end of fear; if you completely surrender your life to the rule of God and believe that whatever happens happens because God is king, you are never afraid of anything. There is released in you vitality that makes for physical as well as spiritual well-being. If, on the other hand, you prefer to be your own ruler and to set your own standards and go your own way, then life will pass you by, and when the Kingdom comes, you will be left in outer darkness.

So, as Jesus talked to the people about the Kingdom, it was a threat to some, to the hard-hearted, to the mean, to the begrudging, to the people who wanted to get back at their enemies, to the people who led narrow, shriveled lives in which there was no grace, no loving kindness whatsoever; the Kingdom was a threat to them, for when the rush of new life should come, they would be passed by and left in desolation.

To Jesus, the Kingdom was the most important thing in the world; it was like a pearl of great price, it was like a treasure buried in a field which a man would give anything to possess. And above everything else, it was at hand, it was just around the corner; some day in the near future it would come suddenly, completely, but it was at hand all the time. And so Jesus went from town to town to tell the people about the Kingdom; it was life, abundant life under the rule of God and all they had to do was accept it. It is no wonder that they heard him gladly. They were astonished at the things he said, and apparently, according to the record, the thing that made the biggest impression upon them was his authority. He did not quote Scripture very often; he seldom referred to authorities to substantiate what he said; he simply stood before them and said, "The Kingdom of God is at hand; repent, believe this good news and enter into the new life." And there was an authority about what he said that stirred them to the very depths.

The service in the synagogue was scarcely over when there was a disturbance in the congregation; a man began to scream. He had an unclean spirit—in those days his mental illness was described in those terms. People did not blame him for what he did; they said, "He is possessed by a devil, he is not himself." When he got up in the congregation and began to scream at Jesus, people were troubled and wondered what Jesus would do. He let the man say what he had to say, then he looked at him and he pointed his finger, and he said to the devils that he himself believed were possessing the man, "Be still! Come out of him!" And there, before the congregation, the man was cured. The devils did come out of him and he was again in his right mind. The people did not know what to think.

Then, after the service, Jesus and his four friends went to the house where they were staying; it happened to be the home of Simon Peter. They were no sooner there when Jesus was told that Peter's mother-in-law was indisposed. Exactly what her illness was we do not know, but it is called "a fever" in the New Testament, apparently not serious, but she was incapacitated. They took Jesus to see the elderly woman, and he stood by her, and spoke to her, and she felt, as hundreds of others felt, the power of his personality; her mind was taken completely off herself and her own indisposition. All her normal resources of health were set in motion, and Jesus took her hand and lifted her up, and the fever disappeared and she went about getting supper for them.

Then we read in the record that the day came to an end in this extraordinary way. "At even, when the sun did set, they brought unto him all that were diseased, and them that were possessed with devils. And all the city was gathered together at the door." And there went out of

Jesus an extraordinary energy that made those people well. The public career of Jesus is there set forth in all its simple strength; it consisted of telling the people about the Kingdom of God and showing them what the Kingdom was like. It was life and health and, above all, love.

When night came, he went to bed, but before daybreak he got up and went out, by himself, into the hills to pray. And Jesus' busy life, as he went about in the towns and villages, was a constant rhythm, to and from the people and back to God. When Simon Peter came looking for him in the morning to get him to go back to Capernaum, to meet more people who had come to see him, Jesus said, "Let us go into the next towns, that I may preach there also: for therefore came I forth." And then this wonderful sentence, which describes in one line the public career of Jesus: "And he went on making the proclamation in the synagogues throughout Galilee, and expelling demons." He went on from town to town telling the people about the Kingdom of God and the life that was theirs for the asking, and showing them what life was like when they came into contact with the power of God.

II

Now, one or two observations on the public career of Jesus. The public career of Jesus was a *ministry*. That is what we call it. In any book on the New Testament you will find this part of the life of Jesus referred to as "the Ministry." He himself said, "The son of man came not to be ministered unto, but to minister." In other words, it is the career of a man who served others. He showed us, I think, as no one else has ever shown us, the sovereignty of service. And is it not true that a man's, or a woman's, career in life amounts to just this: how much use he is to other people? You look at the happy people you know, and in every case they will be people who are ministering in some way to other people. And I say this very directly to you: if you are engaged in a work in which there is no possibility of your putting into that work the element of ministry, get out of it. Life will have no meaning for you unless your public career becomes in some sense a ministry.

The second observation is that the ministry of Jesus began with God and not with men. Jesus did not set out to reform the world, but to reconcile men and women to God. He did not go about the towns and villages to set up a welfare state, but to proclaim the Kingdom of God. And as far as we can tell from the record, it is perfectly clear that Jesus was not so much interested in the rights of man as he was in the rule of God. His ministry was a ministry of the Kingdom of God, and there is the paradoxical fact, he changed the world. He did not create a single welfare agency himself, yet he has inspired every welfare agency. He changed the world by changing the hearts of men and women. I think it is always so. Who is the person in the eighteenth century who accomplished most in the practical way of making life better for men and women? John Wesley, a man who was not interested specifically in reforms at all, but in redeeming the lives of people and inviting them to enter the Kingdom of God. I am afraid we in our time set our goals too near, and our sights too low. There are times when we must be practical; but the real thing is the thing that comes when men have their eyes on the far-off Kingdom, the realm of God which is the rule of God in men's hearts.

And the last observation is that the ministry of Jesus never ended. It did not seem to accomplish anything and yet people remembered what he said; they could never forget him, and after the first shock of the Cross, they began to pick up and go on and to show forth the life of the Kingdom wherever they went; they talked about it all around the Mediterranean basin; they showed people what life was like, and the ministry has gone on until it comes right here to you and to me. And still it goes on.

In 1905, a man stood in Times Square where 42nd Street crosses Broadway, and as he watched the swarm of humanity this is what he wrote:

> *Where cross the crowded ways of life,*
> *Where sound the cries of race and clan,*
> *Above the noise of selfish strife,*
> *We hear thy voice, O Son of man.*
>
> *In haunts of wretchedness and need,*
> *On shadowed thresholds dark with fears,*
> *From paths where hide the lures of greed,*
> *We catch the vision of thy tears.*
>
> *O Master, from the mountain side,*
> *Make haste to heal these hearts of pain;*
> *Among these restless throngs abide,*
> *O tread the city's streets again;*

Till sons of men shall learn thy love,
*   And follow where thy feet have trod;*
Till glorious from thy heav'n above,
*   Shall come the city of our God.**

---

* By F. M. North. Reprinted by permission.

V. THE TRIUMPHAL ENTRY

THE STORY of Jesus now comes rapidly to its climax. After a brief public career in Galilee, Jesus decided to go to Jerusalem. He did not tell his friends why and they did not ask him why. Jerusalem was the religious capital of the nation; if anyone wished to speak to the nation, that was the place to do it. He knew that it would be dangerous. John the Baptist had been beheaded there just a few months before, and prophets down through the centuries had been persecuted and killed in Jerusalem. He knew that the chances were good that he would not come back alive. And yet he was determined to go.

He seemed to be in no great hurry to get there; it was about as far from Galilee to Jerusalem as it is from Albany to New York. He did not go by the direct route, parallel to the river, but across the river and through the hill country on the other side of the Jordan. He took the journey rather leisurely. It took him almost six weeks to get there, and he stopped all along the way to tell the people about the Kingdom and to show them what the Kingdom was like.

He took time with the children, even though the disciples thought that the children ought not to bother him and tried to keep them away. He reproved his disciples and let the children come. He spent time with young men who had serious questions, even though not quite such serious intentions. And he even took time to deal with blind beggars who wanted help.

In other words, wherever Jesus went he ministered to people. His life was all of a piece. You might say he lived all of his life. Some people, you know, live for the week ends, the special occasions, and their working life is like a parenthesis, to be endured and borne only because they can look forward to the bright spots at the end, when they have no responsibilities. Not so with Jesus; Jesus was determined to go to Jerusalem, but he was not so anxious to get there that he ceased to be himself on the way. He ministered all along the way.

I

This part of the story really gets under way when Jesus and his party reach the outskirts of the Holy City. For one thing, it was the great holiday season of the year, the Passover. It was a festival in the Jewish calendar the like of which we do not have. Thanksgiving Day in our calendar comes perhaps nearest to it, for it was both a religious and a national festival. On that day every Jew who possibly could went to Jerusalem as a pilgrim; all the roads going up to Jerusalem from the provinces north and south and even from the east were crowded with pilgrims. The excitement was great, for as they went they sang the songs of Zion: "I was glad when they said unto me, We will go into the house of the Lord"; "I will lift up mine eyes unto the hills." Whatever the road might be, whether a highway or a path coming up from the river, there was a group of pilgrims on it, and as they traveled to the Holy City they sang the songs of their forefathers. So the atmosphere was charged with the excitement of a great holiday season.

Then Jesus did a dramatic thing. Instead of walking into the city he rode, on an ass, which is described in the dictionary as "a long-eared, usually ash-colored, quadruped, of the horse family, when domesticated serving as a slow, patient, sure-footed beast of burden, and proverbial for obstinacy and stupidity, a donkey." Why did Jesus ride into the city instead of walking? He had walked all the way from Galilee, one hundred and fifty miles and more, and now, the last half hour, he chose to ride, and to ride on a donkey.

Some have said that he was tired, that it was a long pull uphill from Jericho, a five-hour journey, climbing three thousand feet in seventeen miles, and that Jesus, exhausted by that uphill climb, rode into the city because he was tired. Possibly, but not probably. Others, following the writer of Matthew's Gospel, say that there was a much more serious reason behind what he did, namely that he was fulfilling the prophecy of Zechariah: "Behold thy king cometh unto thee: lowly, and riding upon an ass." Therefore, the assumption of the evangelist is, although Jesus never said it himself, that he rode into the city the way he did to fulfill the prediction that the Messiah would come that way. Hence, his action was a public demonstration of a new kind of authority and power.

As a matter of fact, we do not really know why he rode into the city. The men who wrote the Gospels, you see, were not so much interested in analyzing Jesus as they were in proclaiming him. And it is very seldom that they try to explain the motives that were behind the things that Jesus did. They seem not at all interested in that, and they content themselves with describing the things he did. Moreover, they often read into the motives of Jesus what came to be their later interpretation of him. By the time they came to write down the Gospel story, Jesus was their king, and it was very easy for them to read into his motives the desire and intention to proclaim himself king on Palm Sunday.

This much, however, we do know. Jesus was dramatic by nature; that was part of his Jewish inheritance. Jesus was much more likely to tell a story than to preach a sermon. Jesus saw the truth about life in the drama of human lives, and not in abstract discourses. He was more like an actor than a professor. When he was about to leave his friends he did not give a farewell address, he did something dramatic. He took bread and wine and gave it to them, and said that it was the symbol of his body and blood which were given for them. We know that much. We expect him to do the dramatic thing.

We also know that the entrance into the city had been very carefully arranged. There is every indication in the story, as all the evangelists tell it, that Jesus had somehow

51

got word to a man who had a donkey and told him to have it at such and such a place at such and such a time; when the little group reached that particular village he told his friends to go on ahead and they would find an ass tied alongside the street, to loose it and bring it to him. If anybody asked them why they were taking the animal, they were to say, "The Lord needs it," and he would let them have it. It was all very carefully planned; there was nothing haphazard or accidental about it.

Furthermore, we know that going into the city as he did, he made it clear, indubitably clear, that he had no political or military moves in mind. Certainly, no one who intended to make an assault upon a city would go into it riding upon a donkey. He went into the city as humbly as he could, in order to make it clear that he came not to be ministered unto but to minister, not to lord it over people but to serve people, and not to condemn people but to love them, so that they could have the life that God was ready and willing to give them.

And finally, we know that the people turned this entry of his into a triumphal procession; they covered the dusty roads with their garments as though they were making a way for a king to travel. They cut down branches from the trees and they brought them to wave before him as he went; and they shouted and yelled, and the shouts were the shouts for a king. "Hosanna," they sang, "save us! Blessed is he that cometh in the name of the Lord! Blessed is the kingdom of our father, David! Hosanna in the highest!" And we can hear the shouts of the Galilean pilgrims, people from his own countryside, who knew him and who loved him and who had confidence in him and great hopes for him; and as he rode on an ass into the city of Jerusalem they gathered round him and made that sad entrance into an indifferent city a triumphant procession.

The story then comes to what seems to us as we read it almost an anticlimax after all the shouting, after all the suggestions of royalty and power and victory and triumph. What did Jesus do when he finally got into the city, after the long journey with all the dangers involved? What did he do? There was no *coup d'état,* there were no pronouncements, no speeches, no soldiers, no challenges to anybody; as a matter of fact, nobody paid much attention. Nothing happened. "And when he had looked round about upon all things, it being now eventide, he went out into Bethany with the twelve." If he came to rule, he surely was a new kind of king who, when he made his way into the capital city, contented himself with a penetrating gaze into the things that were happening in the city, and then went out to spend the night with his friends. That is the story.

II

Now, briefly, what does the story mean? One hesitates to make any comment on it, because the meaning of the story is so obvious and yet so hard to put into words. And yet, one ventures some commentary because, as obvious as the meaning of the story is, it has really been taken in by very few people. It means briefly this: *when Jesus offered his people life they rejected it.* That is what it means. It means that when Jesus offered his people new life, physical, mental, moral, spiritual life, they refused it. This is what he said to them, if we may paraphrase what he said: "If you submit to the rule of God, you will have new life, new health of mind, body, and spirit; but the rule of God is the rule of love, and you cannot have the life unless you are willing to love."

Now the people in Jerusalem were smart enough to know what that meant. They knew that if they followed that and if they accepted what Jesus said, their religion would have to be changed from top to bottom. They knew, for example, that the temple would have to become once more a real temple and not a banking house; that the wealthy hierarchy that controlled the temple would have to become the servants of the people. They knew that their religion would have to be radically revised. Routine performance of religious obligations would have to be replaced by a dedication of spirit to the will of God. And they knew also that the law which meant so much to them would have to be entirely rewritten so that the emphasis was not so much on the performance of things done, the number of services attended, how complete the fast before communion, but upon what they were like inside, and why they did what they did, and what their attitude was toward the people they did not particularly like. Their law would have to be entirely rewritten. There would have to be a place for sinners in it, and also for Gentiles. Moreover, they knew—and this was the thing that was very difficult for them to face—they knew that all their hopes for a military revolt against Rome would have to be forgotten.

They knew that God's rule of love included enemies as well as friends, and that they would have to set aside forever any hope of a rebellion. And they knew that the life of the individual would have to be turned upside down; that he would have to begin to trust God rather than himself; that he would have to try to put God's will before his own will, and that he would have to become like a little child, putting his life in God's hands. It was too much for them, too radical, with too big a price to pay, too much to give up, too many risks to run, too much to lose, and they refused. They rejected the offer.

So there is an infinite sadness about Palm Sunday. It is a strange kind of day in which sadness is so mingled with joy. You see, it is the deep sadness of something glorious and beautiful refused and rejected. There they were, on the threshold of life, yet they refused to go in. So near and yet so far. So wise and yet so foolish. To increase the sadness, the rejection has continued through the years. Person after person, and nation after nation, have not been willing to make the necessary changes in order to accept the rule of God. One hesitates to ask what our nation would do if that promise and offer were made to it.

And yet, mingled with the sadness of the day, there is still some of the joy of that first Palm Sunday, for the royal figure of Jesus is still somehow mysteriously before us. In spite of rejection after rejection, that royal figure still goes on before us, still haunting our memories and challenging our hopes and stimulating our spirits and our courage. After all these years and all these failures on our part to accept what he has to give us, he still makes the promise, and I wish through me he could make that promise to you and to our nation. If you are willing to submit to the rule of God, God will give you new life; but the rule of God is the rule of love, and you cannot have the life unless you are willing to love. Will you accept that? Will you take the chance? That is the promise, that is the offer, and it is up to you to decide.

Once to ev'ry man and nation
Comes the moment to decide,
In the strife of truth with falsehood,
For the good or evil side;
Some great cause, God's new Messiah,
Off'ring each the bloom or blight,
And the choice goes by forever
'Twixt that darkness and that light.

By the light of burning martyrs
Jesus' bleeding feet I track,
Toiling up new Calvaries ever
With the cross that turns not back;
New occasions teach new duties,
Time makes ancient good uncouth;
They must upward still and onward
Who would keep abreast of truth.

VI. THE LAST SUPPER

THE NEXT chapter in the story is about a meal. The meal did not take place in Rome, which was the center of civilization in those days, but in one of the condemned cities of the world, Jerusalem. Forty years after the meal took place the city was laid in ruins, and has been a virtual battlefield ever since.

The meal did not take place in a palace, one of the earth's great houses, but in the upper room of a house of which we know neither the name of the owner, nor the condition, nor the address. There were thirteen people present at the meal, and only one of them had any public reputation at all; even he was not known beyond a radius of a hundred and fifty miles from his home town, and he was killed the day after the meal as a disturber of the peace. The other people who attended the meal were young laboring men whom nobody had ever heard of before or ever expected to see again. It was not a banquet; it consisted of the bare necessities of life, bread and wine.

And yet, this meal, so hidden, so apart from the great

stream of events, so obscure, so apparently local and transient, this meal is now being celebrated and remembered and participated in by people in practically every country in the world. That is an extraordinary fact, and the question it raises in our mind is this: What gave this meal its lasting quality and its spreading power? Wherein lies the perennial appeal of this meal whereby it can speak to men and women in all walks of life, through almost two thousand years of time, in very different circumstances and conditions of life?

I

Before we answer that question let us pause long enough to make this observation. Events that seem unimportant to us at the time often turn out to be the hinges upon which swing the doors into the future. No one, certainly, would have predicted on that night on which the Last Supper took place that of all the things going on in the city of Jerusalem that night, that meal would be the one thing to be most often remembered down through the years. For one thing, it was the time of the great Passover festival, the keystone of the Jewish year, the great holiday of deliverance. People came from all over to celebrate this great festival; the best people were there, the greatest minds, the profoundest spirits were gathered together in Jerusalem. Moreover, Pilate was in town. He was the governor representing the occupying power, and since Herod was not very far away, undoubtedly affairs of state were taking place in the city which might have to do with the rise and fall of nations. And yet none of these affairs conquered time. In fact, we know about them only as they happen to relate and refer themselves to this meal. Rather, it is a little undistinguished group of young men having supper together under the threat of doom that has conquered time.

You never know where the seeds of life may be lying. If you have a baby, he may become the saviour of his people. If you eat a meal, it may become, in the course of time, a sacrament of salvation. If you say something, something that seems perhaps unimportant and insignificant at the time, it may save a life, or destroy one. If you make a decision, it may turn the tide of history. If you start an idea going, it may change the course of human life for generations to come. And if you die, you may accomplish more than you would have accomplished if you had lived. In other words, nothing in life is unimportant, at least in this sense: all life is loaded with possibilities. Not all of them are explored, not all of them materialize, not all of them reach maturity, but we as Christians, taking part in this extraordinary meal which seemed so unimportant, insignificant, and irrelevant at the time, are reminded that the material of our lives is of the most intense significance, even the most minute details of it, for it is all charged with the possibilities of God.

You say, "Not in my case. Nothing that I could do, nothing that I could take part in, could possibly be as important as that. I'm just an unimportant person who has no position in life, casts no deciding vote, and spreads no great influence. Certainly it's not true in my case." But I ask you, what would Peter have said if somebody had asked him on the Thursday night before Good Friday what he thought about the Last Supper? What would he have said in answer to someone who said, "You have just taken part in a meal that will be through the generations the center of men's worship and the incentive of their living"? He would have said, "Poppycock!"

II

Now let us get back to our first question. What gives this particular meal its lasting quality? My mind goes at once to two things, two reasons for the perennial appeal of this meal. I am sure there are others.

First, the people who knew Jesus wanted something to remember him by. Human memory is one of the most mysterious of our faculties, and one of the most wonderful, and it can reach back through the years that are gone and pluck things out of the past and make them vivid. But at best, the human memory fades as the years go by, and even people we have known well and loved deeply have a way of slipping from our immediate consciousness. It must have been so with Jesus, and the people who knew him did not want to forget him. They wanted something to remember him by, and they found it in this meal.

For one thing, it was so like him. It seemed to epitomize, in brief, dramatic, direct action and word everything that he had said and done and been. It was simple, not complex; that was characteristic of Jesus, always simple, direct, never complicating issues with irrelevant facts and ideas that might be interesting but not to the point. So, this meal went right to the point in question. Like him, it was concrete, not abstract. And even more like him it was plain, so plain that the simplest person could grasp it; yet it was not crude. Jesus had a unique way of being able to be unmistakably plain, yet never cheap and never vulgar.

Also, like him, the meal was somehow entirely surrounded by God; when it began he gave thanks; when it ended they went out on the Mount of Olives and sang a hymn. Also, it made his followers think of him because it had to do with bread and breakage. It had to do with bread because bread was the very stuff of physical existence and Jesus never tried to skirt those necessities. But the bread he gave to his disciples was broken bread; it was not the promise of a perfect body; it was not the ideal of the Greek body without flaw or blemish of any kind; it was a body broken, scarred, marred, tortured, through which the glory of the infinite came. Bread and breakage, life and death—the two things that concerned Jesus all his life.

The first Christians, then, turned to this meal. It is interesting to notice that they did not remember Jesus in those first days so much by the last words that he spoke, although they preserved those; they remembered him chiefly by the last supper that he ate. Again, characteristically, action before words.

But there is another reason for the perennial appeal of the Last Supper. The Last Supper condensed the meaning of life and death into unmistakable and comprehensible terms—not only for the people who lived with Jesus in Palestine but for people all down through the ages, and in the ages to come, for whom the questions of life and death will be essentially the same questions that he and his contemporaries had to face, and that you and I have to face. Some people have given men and women a discourse on the meaning of life and death in an attempt to answer those questions. Jesus gave them, rather, a simple act in which they could take part, and as we take part in it again, we shall perhaps be conscious of the way in which it condenses the meaning of life and answers some of the questions we ask.

For instance, in some way or other, in either an articulate way or an unspoken way, all of us ask the question, "Does anybody really care about me? My friends have done their bit and my family has shown me their love and affection. But does anything at the heart of things care whether I live or die, or am happy or unhappy, or make the most of life or a mess of life? Does anybody care?" Then the words of Jesus come to us: "This is my body which is given for you," and we take it in our hands, and we feel it, and somehow or other we know that somebody cares that much. Some ask the question, "Can my sins ever be blotted out?" No matter how sophisticated we may be, no matter how conditioned we may be to the idea of sin as a part of human nature, nevertheless we do not like our sins and we are not proud of them. And there comes a time in everyone's life when he says, "Can these mistakes that I see so plainly now, these wrongs, these sins, can anything be done to offset them in the balance of life?" And the words come, "My blood was shed for the remission of your sins." Don't ask how. The mystery of one man's sacrifice outweighing the balance of all men's sins is not for our analysis. When we hear the words and see the cup and drink the wine, somehow or other we have the assurance that our sins are forgiven.

Many of us at one time or another ask the question, "Have I anything in common with my neighbor? In this extraordinarily social world in which I live, often in close contact with people I don't particularly like, who do not share my point of view, not only religiously but politically, who seem to me to be miles apart from anything that I ever am or hope to be, have I anything in common with my neighbor?" And we come to the altar rail and we realize that we have in common our empty hands; the needs that are common to all of us; the empty part of our lives that must be filled with a life outside ourselves if there is to be any life at all. We have these things in common with all men as we raise our empty hands to receive the bread.

And some people ask from time to time, "Is there anything for me to do in the world? I don't seem to count very much; I haven't any position of great importance; I don't exert much influence in the world, and I sometimes feel that I'm a pretty useless person. Is there anything for me to do in the world?" "Do this in remembrance of me," comes the answer. "Do in your own imperfect and inadequate way the thing that I did. Let the glory shine through the breakage, that men may be able to pick up the pieces of their lives and live better lives because of you."

And finally, I am sure that most people at some time during their lives are likely to ask, "In the darkness of my night is there anyone with me, or in this darkness am I alone, isolated, a forlorn and forsaken figure without help or companionship or strength?" And the words, "In the night in which he was betrayed he took bread," come to us, and we feel him with us in the night, and we say, "Then shall my night be turned to day."

In 1904 James Bisset Pratt was a student of philosophy; he later became, as many of you know, the great and beloved professor of philosophy at Williams College. In 1904 he did what a great many students desire to do: he got up a questionnaire and sent it to all the leading philosophers of his day. He asked questions like these: "Why do you believe in God? Do you pray, and if so, why? Do you believe in personal immortality?" One of the philosophers to whom he sent the questionnaire was William James. William James answered all the questions rather carefully. When he came to this item, "Describe a typical spiritual person," he put down, "Phillips Brooks." Certainly, no one could have been better qualified than William James was to describe a spiritual person; but he knew that mere description would not mean much to anybody, for the abstract realities of spiritual life are known and understood only as they become concrete in something real, a person.

Sometimes when people ask us to describe the meaning of life, its joy and sorrow, suffering and tragedy, we feel that while we perhaps might do it in an abstract discourse on the meaning of existence, we can do it much more plainly, much more completely by saying simply, "the Last Supper—that is the meaning of life, the bread and the breakage, and the Life."

Of course, as the years have passed, the meal has become more and more formal. Some people object to that and are inclined to say, "Well, the simplicity of that first meal has been lost, lost in ceremony and ritual formality and liturgy." It is, I think, bound to be so, for if you think a minute you will see that a certain amount of formality is necessary to protect the things that we care most about. A wedding, for instance, is not a casual, careless performance but is surrounded by a certain amount of formality. The graduation of a boy or girl from college is not an indifferent affair; it is surrounded by simple ritual; the inauguration of a president, the burial of a person are performed with a care for detail and pattern. Ritual protects these things, shields them from carelessness and lack of reverence. And so it is only natural that a certain amount of formality has grown up around this meal, more in some traditions than in others.

My final word is this: never let the formality, however necessary, hide the reality of what is taking place. This is the reality that is acted out in dramatic terms in this meal of which you are now a part. To live is to give; to give is to suffer; to suffer is to die; to die to self is to live.

VII. THE CROSS

WE HAVE been following the story of Jesus with little reference to ourselves or our lives; of course, we were bound to think of ourselves as we followed that story, but we have not been preoccupied with our own concerns, or our problems and anxieties. We have tried to focus our attention on something quite apart from us, as a man looks at a masterpiece. And now on Good Friday that story leads into the story of the Cross.

Before we begin the story of the Cross, I should like to point out one or two things that may help you appreciate that story. In the first place, it is a very old story. You have all heard it hundreds of times. You know the details of it by heart; we preachers have told the story many, many times, and you might almost think that it would become hackneyed and trite and obvious. But it never does.

One reason for this is that it is a story of conflict, indeed the major conflict of life, the conflict between good and evil, the conflict between darkness and light, the conflict between life and death. And we all have our share of conflict. We have conflicts within ourselves, conflicts between the person we should like to be and the person we know we really are; we have conflicts between ourselves and our environment, our society and our world order and our civilization, and the demands they make upon us. We have family conflicts where will crosses will, just as the beams of the Cross crossed each other. So we have a particular interest in this story because of the nature of it. It is the story of a conflict, and conflicts concern us because we are so continually involved in them.

Then, of course, it is not only the story of a conflict but also the story of a conquest. It is the story of how the major conflict between good and evil was somehow not resolved, not eliminated, not escaped, not avoided, but redeemed, overcome, transcended. Thus the story gives us, in words we cannot define and cannot always understand or phrase specifically, the assurance that the conflicts in ourselves and the conflicts that exist between ourselves and the outside world can be conquered, that they need not end in frustration or defeat or despair, that there is a way to handle them. It has been done. And in setting forth this story once again, we shall try to keep before us not only the conflict but the mighty conquest.

One thing we must be sure to take into consideration, and about which we should perhaps be on our guard, is that we are more than spectators at a great drama—though we are in such a position. It was the spectators at the great Greek tragedies who were purged of their impurities because of what they saw. But this story goes beyond that; it is more than a spectacle that we witness and perhaps enjoy and revel in emotionally. This is a story that we in some sense take part in. It is in a real sense the story of every man's life. It is the story of every man's suffering and temptation, and testing and agony, and hope, and faith, and death, and life. So that as you read the story I hope you will make an honest effort to project yourself into it. As you watch Peter in that dramatic episode that we will read about a little later, perhaps you will see yourself in Peter. Perhaps you will ask yourself, "What is there of that in me?" As you leave the story, you may be a different person from what you were when you began. In other words, you want something to happen to you while you read it. You turn to it not simply to enjoy a spectacle or to indulge your grief. Jesus does not need your grief. You remember what he said to the women of Jerusalem, "Weep not for me; I don't need your tears; weep for yourselves and for your children."

And so, while we are focusing our attention on something entirely outside ourselves, something objective, something that once happened, not a fancy, not a fiction, but a fact, we are all the time projecting ourselves into that story. "Where am I in this scene? What is there of Pilate in me, or of Judas, or of Peter, and the rest?" If we are able to do that, then this will not be just another telling of the story, but it may be the means of helping us manage our conflicts better, of increasing the number of our conquests over ourselves and our environment.

VIII. THE ARREST

THE STORY of the Cross begins, properly speaking, with the arrest of Jesus. Jesus had been relatively successful in Galilee, there in the north province, in his own home country. He had from the very beginning a large popular following, and I think we should mark the fact that the Jewish people themselves did not kill Jesus. The majority of the Jewish people who knew him loved him, followed him for various reasons, some more seriously than others, but it was the leaders who were against him from the start. Even when he was in Galilee they were spying on him to see what he was doing, and they made it so difficult for him that finally he had to leave.

Now he was in Jerusalem at the time of the Passover festival and he was completely exposed to the people. By the way in which he had entered the city on Palm Sunday he had declared himself to everyone, and the leaders were out to get him. Naturally, they wanted to do it as quickly and quietly as possible, for they, like all other leaders then and now, did not want to create a disturbance. They were willing to do almost anything to keep things quiet. They did not want to make trouble; they did not want to inconvenience themselves and they did not want to do anything that would upset the equilibrium between the local governors and the Roman government. So, they were seeking to arrest him by stealth.

The arrest, therefore, was made at night. They did not dare to do it in the daylight. The obvious reason, of course, is that they were afraid of the people. Jesus had too many friends in Jerusalem. There would have been too much danger of a public uprising. We wonder as we read the story—and we are of course permitted to use our imagination and to read between the lines here and there—whether they were not only afraid of the people but also ashamed of themselves. Evil has at least this much modesty, that it shrinks from the light. There are some people who are brash enough to go ahead with their deviltry in the daylight, but most people are not so. And it is easy to imagine that the leaders in this case were people who would just as soon do what they did in the darkness. It would be hard for most people to betray a friend, for instance, in broad daylight, not so much for the danger it might put them in, but because they do not want to look at themselves. We all do things in the dark that we would not do in the light.

Not only do we seek the absence of light when we want to do things that we would not normally do, but we often in these days seek the absence of identity. We go out looking for the darkness of anonymity. Our great cities are filled with people who have gravitated to them because no one knows them there, and they can do things there in the darkness of their anonymity that they would never dream of doing in the broad daylight of Main Street in their home town. Now certainly every man has a right to some privacy, and there are things we all do that are better done behind closed doors; but when a man begins to seek the cover of darkness, then he had better take care. When we find we want to do things that we could not do in the open light of day, we had better begin to ask ourselves some questions.

The word of Jesus has come down across the centuries and it seems to me it comes upon us today with an unequaled seriousness. "This is your hour, and the power of darkness." And so it was, for what they had to do they would not have the face to do in the daylight. They had at least that much decency.

Moreover this arrest was made in a garden. The name of the garden was Gethsemane. I do not like to pause too often in the interest of rather irrelevant details, but it occurs to me each year as I read the Gospels during Lent that the names of places have an unusual beauty of sound. Gethsemane. We shall come to others. This particular word means "oil press," and the reason the garden was named that seems obvious. There was a grove of olive trees near by on the slopes of the Mount of Olives. The olives were brought to the press and the oil was pressed out. There are many overtones here on which the imagination might dwell for considerable time; but let us remember that it is the press from which the precious things of life finally come.

Why not in some public place? Jesus himself said to the people who came from him, "I was daily with you in the temple teaching and ye took me not." There again they were afraid of his popularity and they were obsessed with the idea that nothing must be done to disturb the peace or to upset the city. And, especially, nothing must be done to upset the Roman governor. So, when they laid hands on him to take him they did it behind the walls of a garden.

Evil seems to stop at nothing. It is amazing, when you stop to think of it, that no walls can keep it out. No beauty daunts it. You might think that the very nature of a garden would deter men from such a deed, but not at all. The walls did not keep them out. The beauty did not stop them, for evil has a way of making its way right into the heart of life, and sometimes it seems that the more beautiful a rose is the more likely you are to find a canker at the center of it. Evil makes its way into the most sacred parts of our lives. It may be of some help to us while we are thinking quietly about Good Friday to reckon with the fact that evil does not respect even the walls of a man's home. How many times you and I have seen homes that seem to be model homes of family life and we say to ourselves, "Surely those walls would never admit anything evil." And then we hear that disease has stricken one of the sons in that family.

Or, much more tragic, we hear that moral evil has wormed its way into the very heart of a family. No one is immune. Not even a church. You might think that the sacred walls of a church would keep evil out, but those of us who spend a good deal of time in church know that those walls cannot do that, that those of us in the church are, it sometimes seems, in a way more susceptible to pride and vanity and envy than people who are outside. And it is true of an **indivi**dual life, a life that looks fine and fair and free; you say to yourself, "Nothing can ever attack that life." And yet at some unguarded moment evil makes its way into it.

Worst of all, of course, was the fact that the arrest was made while Jesus was praying. Even a less noble man than Hamlet would have hesitated to lay hands on a man while he was praying, but not so in this case.

Jesus apparently had come to the garden for the specific purpose of praying. He knew in a certain sense what he was facing and he was gathering his resources at the fountainhead of strength. He had come there to take his direction once again and to be sure of his way. He told his three close friends that he was sorrowful and sore troubled and when he knelt down to pray he asked God to remove the cup from him. It is one of the great scenes in the history of mankind.

How many nameless people have prayed the same prayer? They have been aware of the fact that there was ahead of them some difficult thing to do, some great pain to endure, some hard crisis to go through, and they have got down on their knees and said, "O Lord, take this cup away from me." Jesus did the same thing. He prayed that God might remove the cup, and God did not remove it. At the time, there was no good answer to the question why God did not take the cup away. All we know is—and it is certainly worth repeating—that God did not take away the cup; but he gave Jesus the grace to drink the cup in such a way as to take the bitterness out of all the cups of pain from that day to this. There may be times when God will not take away your cup and all he will give you is the strength to take what is in it, and when you take it, it will disappear. If we could learn that, and live by it, and trust it, our lives would be brighter, freer, and far, far more creative.

Finally, the arrest, made under the cover of darkness, in

the privacy of a garden, while Jesus was saying his prayers, was led by one of his own friends. See how the tragedy increases. Judas had turned against him. We do not know why. There has been a great deal of speculation about it. It seems hard to think that Judas was an out and out rotter. Jesus was pretty shrewd about men and it seems unlikely that he would have chosen Judas if he had not known that he had good stuff in him.

It is hard to believe that Judas betrayed Jesus for the little money that he got out of it. It was hardly worth it, although some men have done less evil for less money. As we look at Judas it seems more likely that he was fed up with the whole business. Jesus was too slow for him, the way to Calvary too long. It would never work. And, as Judas looked at the situation with his practical eye, he came to the point where he said to himself, "The meek will never inherit the earth and we might as well admit it now." In other words, Judas may have been the kind of person who becomes tired of being good, patient, and understanding. Do you ever feel that way? I do. You get to the point where you say, "It isn't worth it. I have tried and tried to be understanding and loving and charitable, and I'm tired, I'm weary, and it doesn't work, and I don't think it ever will work, and I'm fed up with the whole business."

At any rate, Judas sold himself to the leaders to be used in their crafty scheme. And he came that night to the garden. The moon was probably out, for it was the time of the Passover full moon. He was at the head of a motley group of men from the high priest's house, and the amazing thing is that they came equipped with clubs and swords. There was just about as much chance of destroying Jesus with clubs and swords as there is of destroying the moonlight with a machine gun. Spiritual realities in life are never destroyed by physical forces. And what fools these men made of themselves.

Jesus said to them, "Are you come out as against a brigand with clubs and swords and staves? I was right there with you. Why didn't you take me?" And then Judas went up to Jesus and kissed him. It was the agreed-upon signal and the men who were behind Judas then went and laid hands on Jesus and took him.

But the important thing in the picture, as in all the scenes we recount, is the way in which Jesus behaved. Here he was in the garden praying and one of his friends came leading a group of men to arrest him, and when Judas kissed him, Jesus turned and said to him, "My friend, do that for which thou art come." It seems to me that all the love and grace of a million years are in that salutation, "My friend." Not a word of self-defense or rebuff.

So we can say that while it is true that evil can make its way into every walled garden of life, the one place where evil never succeeded in settling was in the spirit of Jesus. And even though he was arrested, Jesus was still as free as the wind.

IX. HEARING
BEFORE
CAIAPHAS

Now we move on in the story of the Cross to the trial before the high priest. "They led Jesus away to the high priest, and with him were assembled all the chief priests and the elders and the scribes." The high priest in this case was Caiaphas. You all know him, at least by name. He was what we should call the head of the church. When in these chapters I speak of the church instead of the synagogue, I do it simply to make sure that you understand emotionally what group I am talking about. It is very easy to put a blame on the synagogue that we should not like to attach to the church. What we are talking about is institutional religion, and Caiaphas was the head of it in those days.

He was the head of it partly by family inheritance and partly by political appointment, so there was a kind of liaison between the Roman governor and the high priest. It was a position of power and wealth. And he bore the title that many men have proudly borne, the Defender of the Faith. The men with him were the members of the Sanhedrin. That was what we might call the Jewish supreme court. The one in Jerusalem was the largest, with seventy-one members; other towns had their own Sanhedrins. The men in this Sanhedrin represented the aristocracy. They were self-perpetuating, as far as we can see. When one of them died or retired, they appointed another prominent member of the community. They had to do with local, especially religious, matters. At the time of Christ they had no jurisdiction outside Judea; that is the reason they could not do anything about Jesus so long as he was in Galilee, and that is the reason why we said that he was deliberately exposing himself when he went to Jerusalem, because he knew then he came under the jurisdiction of the Sanhedrin.

We have to admit the fact that there was no real trial. In the first place, it was an unearthly hour, before daybreak. There was not a quorum present. The hearing was not held in the usual place. It was more like an examination of Jesus before the high priest and some of his close associates whom he could get together quickly early in the morning. They wanted to get on with the job.

The charge against Jesus was blasphemy. We who blaspheme so casually find it difficult perhaps to realize how serious blasphemy was to a Jew. They took the name of God so seriously that they never even pronounced it, much less took it in vain as an oath. We might define blasphemy, in order to enlarge the range of it slightly, as presumption in the presence of God. Blasphemy is the attempt on the part of a man to do and to be and to have things that are rightly associated only with God.

We must also admit that according to their understanding of blasphemy the Jews had some ground for this charge, because Jesus, you remember, had presumed to forgive sins, and that power belonged only to God. Furthermore, he had

77

presumed to criticize the temple, and for the people the temple was the very center of God's life. To criticize the temple was like criticizing the Lord God himself. And also, he had presumed to supercede the Divine Mosaic law. It is equally hard for us to appreciate that, because we do not take any law very seriously these days. But to the Jews this law was a sacred law; it was the law of Moses. Jesus came and said, "You have heard in the past the law of Moses, but I say unto you. . . ."

At this examination they made a pretense of securing witnesses. They wanted to keep the rules, and the Jewish rules were that there had to be at least two witnesses against a man and their testimony had to agree. But as so often happens, the witnesses did not tell the truth. They claimed that Jesus had said that he would destroy the temple and build it again in three days. He had not said any such thing. He had said something about the destruction of the temple as his disciples marveled at it when they went into Jerusalem, and warned them not to take it too seriously because even things as wonderful as the temple were susceptible to the ravages of time, and he knew that it would not be there too long.

This makes us think of the irresponsible judgments that we make on other people. We misquote other people; we quote them inaccurately and carelessly and do not seem to realize that that kind of irresponsible, careless talk hurts people. In this case it sent the young Prince of glory to death. Remember that when you are tempted to pass around bits of gossip about other people that as far as you know are not founded on any fact whatsoever.

Not only did the witnesses not tell the truth, but they did

not agree. Of course, we know that no two people ever see the same thing exactly the same way. If you and I should witness an accident we should not describe it exactly the same way because we have different eyes. We are prepared for that.

But, you see, there is something deeper involved here. Dishonesty always leads to confusion. When you once start to tell a lie, you tell another, and your lies never agree. And that was the trouble that these people got into. They were not telling the truth and of course they did not agree, because no two people are likely to tell the same lie. Furthermore, and this is an even more serious point to consider, as these men listened to the witnesses their minds were already made up. They did not really want to know the facts. They were not really interested in what the witnesses were saying. They wanted to get rid of Jesus and they were going to do it regardless of what the witnesses said.

How we prejudice the public figures of our day. Our minds are made up ahead of time about the people we do not like, especially people in public office, and no matter what facts were set before us, we still would not like them. I suppose the same thing is true in reverse. There are people we *do* like and even though some serious error they have made is put before us, we still go right on liking them.

How we do start out with foregone conclusions about religion and life, for instance. I meet people every once in a while who say, "I have no use whatsoever for the church." They are not interested in facts and it would not make any difference to them what evidence you put before them. They have made up their minds and that is the end of it. Other people, especially young people, are likely to say,

"Religion is nothing but a relic of antiquity." They decided that a long time ago and evidence is the furthest thing from their minds. Other people sometimes say, "Why, immortality is nothing but a myth," but as far as looking at the evidence or listening to it, they are no more prepared to do that than the men of the Sanhedrin were prepared to examine the evidence about Jesus. But nevertheless, for the sake of decency, they did have witnesses.

When Jesus said nothing, Caiaphas, the chief priest, who had not had much experience with this kind of person, said to him, "Have you no answer to make? What is it that these men testify against you?" But Jesus was silent and made no answer.

Think for a moment about the silence of Jesus—the silence not of stupidity but of a wisdom too deep for words. He had had his say and how gloriously he had said it. "Blessed are the pure in heart: for they shall see God." "A certain man had two sons." "A certain man went down from Jerusalem to Jericho, and fell among thieves." "He that humbleth himself shall be exalted." He had had his say, and there was nothing more to say now in these circumstances. He knew perfectly well that no matter what he said, it would make no difference to the people who were listening. His was not the silence of cowardice, but the silence of courage. There is a time in life to speak and a time to keep still, and if we only knew which was which. If only some parents in a crisis with their children knew when to keep still. Or if we in times of hot-headed anger only knew when to keep still. If, in our prayers beseeching the Lord God for things that we think we need or deserve or should have, we only knew when to keep still.

Caiaphas in desperation said to him, "Art thou the Christ, the Son of the blessed?" (that is, the Messiah), and Jesus said, "I am." Caiaphas said, "You have heard the blasphemy. What need we of further witnesses?" And they all condemned him to death.

Let me suggest two things to consider here. One is the irony of the situation. They thought they were judging Jesus. Think of it. There he was, a peasant from the provinces who had never been heard of until he arrived in the city, being condemned by the highest tribunal in the land. How sure they were that they were right, and how smug. And yet how those figures wither and wilt under the judgment of Jesus. How silly some of us look as we sit around trying to decide what we think about Jesus. Student discussion groups are wonderful things and healthy things but sometimes you want to get up and say, "How presumptuous for young, untrained upstarts to be sitting here discussing what they think about Jesus and saying that they think this, that, or the other thing, when the important thing is what Jesus thinks about them." It is as though we were trying to decide whether it would be beneficial or harmful to the earth for the sun to come up tomorrow morning. It will come, willy-nilly, no matter what the professors or sophomores or churchmen think about it. And so Jesus will come.

The real conflict here, of course, is the conflict between the religion of Caiaphas and the religion of Jesus. Let us look for just a minute at those two contrasting religions, for here is an issue that concerns us who are members of the church. The religion of Caiaphas was locked up in a building. The religion of Jesus was out in the open air where people lived. The religion of Caiaphas was carefully performed in ritual and ceremony. The religion of Jesus was obedience and love. The religion of Caiaphas was wrapped up in the grave-clothes of the past. The religion of Jesus was stripped for action in the present. The religion of Caiaphas was highly organized, like a piece of fine machinery. The religion of Jesus was an unimaginably loosely knit, informal fellowship of people who wanted to be with him. The religion of Caiaphas was concerned with rubrics and canons. The religion of Jesus was concerned with human need and sin.

How many times has professional, institutional religion crushed the tender, free religion of Jesus. As we leave the scene in the high priest's house, with all these things in our minds, I should like to leave with you and impress upon you the thought that over the high priest's house, in all the tumult and excitement, broods the silence of the condemned man.

X. THE DENIAL

WE COME now to another chapter in the story of the Cross that is very close to the life of all of us. While Jesus was being examined in the high priest's house, Peter was outside in the courtyard. He had followed at a safe distance and was warming himself by the fire. It was a natural thing to do. It may have been cool and Peter was probably glad to feel the warmth of the fire in the courtyard, and the safety of it. A great deal has been made of the fact that Peter followed "afar off" and the distance of his following has come to be almost the measure of his disgrace. The important thing is that the rest of the disciples did not follow at all. None of the others followed even at a distance. We do not know where they went. "They all forsook him and fled." And while we do not want to excuse either ourselves or Peter—and we certainly do not want to put ourselves in the position of making things easy, for an easy Christianity never wins anyone—nevertheless, it is better, isn't it, to follow Jesus afar off than not to follow him at all?

Sometimes people tell me that they hesitate to join the

church because they are not good enough. All the more reason why they should join it. It is better, isn't it, to make a stab at the Christian way of life, and fail, than not to try at all?

Then, in the midst of this quiet scene in the courtyard, Peter was cross-examined as Jesus was being examined up above by more important people. A maid came up to Peter and said, "You were there with that man from Nazareth." Peter said, "Why I don't even know him. I don't know whom you are talking about." A little later the maid came again and said to one of the bystanders, "He is one of those people from Galilee." Peter denied it. And later another one came and said, "Of course you are one of them; you are a Galilean, aren't you?" Peter said, "I do not know this man that you are talking about." And outside a cock crew.

Jesus, interestingly enough, had warned Peter just a little while before that this would happen. After the Last Supper, Jesus predicted that they would all lose confidence in him. Contrary to what we sometimes think, Jesus was not over-optimistic about human nature. He said he was talking to "an evil and adulterous generation." He knew that his disciples would desert him, that one of them would betray him, that one of them would deny him, and he was not under any illusions about human nature. He knew that they were well-meaning but weak. And I wonder if he did not know it partly from his own experience.

A line supposedly addressed to Peter, but more likely addressed to the three men who were present at the time, came to me recently with a new meaning. It was spoken by Jesus in the garden; after he left them to watch and went to pray in his agony, he came back and found them asleep.

He said, "Pray that you may not have to go through a testing-time like this because the spirit is willing but the flesh is weak." And I wonder if he was not talking about his own testing-time. From his own experience he knew that though his spirit was alive and alert and willing, the flesh was not so ready until he had mastered it. And he warned Peter of that. When he went on to say that he knew all of them would forsake him, Peter, you remember, protested loudly and said, "Not I! I wouldn't forsake you no matter what happened. You can always count on me." Peter was just a little too sure of himself.

The same thing is true of us. As I said, we are always referring this story to ourselves. We see, for instance, someone who has done something wrong, and we say to ourselves secretly and rather smugly, "I would never have done that." We say to ourselves, "If I were President of the United States, I would appoint men who were honest." Don't be too sure. Or we look at a girl and say, "If I were that girl, I would have stuck by my husband." Don't be too sure. Or we look at a man and we say, "If I were that man I would have the courage to go out and work and earn an honest living." Don't be too sure of yourself. You might, and you might not.

Of course, those of us who are more or less analytical by nature are bound to ask as we look at Peter and watch this scene of the denial, "How could Peter have done it?" It is not so hard for us to understand Judas because we do not know much about him, but we have such a warm feeling for Peter that we wonder how he could have done what he did. Again, we must use our imagination and our judgment as reverently as possible.

For one thing, he was tired. He had been through a long, tense, difficult period. We know our moral resources and physical reserves are very closely related, and we do things sometimes when our physical reserves are low that we should never do if they were up to par. This does not mean, of course, that there are not some people who in the most utter poverty of physical reserve do heroic things morally and spiritually, but it does mean that we can make an allowance for people who do disappointing things when they are physically exhausted. And when we judge people who disappoint us, we should ask the question, "Well, are they tired? Are they up to their physical par?"

Another consideration, of course, is that Peter spoke before he thought. The natural impulse is the impulse to protect ourselves. We all have it. It is part of our very nature, and when someone threatens our safety, we do not stop to think; we hit, we run, we strike. It is true, is it not, that impulse is quicker than intellect? And how much harm do you suppose has been done by people who have acted on impulse before their intellect was able to get into motion and check that impulse? Just think about your own lives. Of course, I cannot speak to you as an individual. But think of what you have done on the impulse of anger. You fly off the handle and say something you would never dream of saying if you had stopped to think. More serious is the impulse to lust. Many tragedies are written of people who have done things on the impulse of the moment, without stopping to think what their action might mean.

Peter was all alone in a hostile company and that, too, I think, made it more difficult for him to be himself and maintain his highest level of behavior. This is true of all of us. It is easy for us to be loyal Americans in our own city, but if we were in Moscow it might not be so easy. It is easy for us to be loyal, outspoken Christians in a group of church people, but when we get in a group of worldly pagans it is not quite so easy. And sometimes even we clergy, when we are in a hostile group—not a violent group but a group we know does not agree with us and is not sympathetic—make that mistake and deny our God.

So Peter denied him. The others, to be sure, did not. They did not even put themselves in a position to be disloyal. They did not have any opportunity to deny him because they saw to it that they were in a place of safety where there was no likelihood of their doing such a thing as that.

Luke has a great line that has been used as the heart of sermons so often that I almost hesitate to mention it: "And the Lord turned and looked upon Peter." We are tempted to let our imagination run over the scene. What do you suppose was in that look of Jesus? To be sure, it was a look of disappointment, I have no doubt about that, and a look of judgment. It could not have been anything else but that at first. But I often wonder whether there was not some delight in that look, delight that somebody was there that he knew, the only person there, during the entire time, who was a friend of his. And while he must have been disappointed in the way Peter had behaved, we cannot help but wonder whether he was not glad to see him just the same.

I am sure that there was in that look a great understanding, as though he had said to Peter, "Peter, you have made an awful mess, but I love you just the same." That, you know, is the look of God. An understanding like that is the understanding of God, not of man. Let that look search you in all the crannies and crevices in which you hide your mistakes and your failures, the things you are ashamed of, and let it cleanse you with its obvious sign of disappointment and judgment. But do not fail to recognize the understanding there. "I love you just the same."

"Peter went out and wept bitterly," or, in other translations, "Peter burst into tears." One has it that Peter "broke down and wept." There were two Peters: there was the real Peter and there was the impulsive Peter who denied Jesus. And the conflict here, since this is a story of conflict, was the conflict between the two. We all know, better than we like to admit, what that conflict is like, because we all have within ourselves two potential people, the person who acts upon impulse and does things he would never do if he stopped to think, and the person who is always wanting to be better than he is.

When that conflict is more than you can bear, when it seems to threaten to break you almost in two, remember what happened to Peter. From that moment, when he was about as far down at the bottom of the pit as anybody could possibly be, Peter began to rise. He was the one who led the way back to Galilee. He was the first one to whom Jesus appeared. He braved the hostility of the crowd on Pentecost. He bore the imprisonments and the persecutions without a word, and, above everything else, when he went to Rome he began to tell the story of Jesus. It is Peter's story, recorded by Mark, that we are now telling. In that story, Peter had both the nobility and the humility to include this incident about himself, as though he were telling those who

considered themselves failures how he once had failed.
What he is saying is this: "Don't be afraid and don't be discouraged when you make a terrible mistake and hurt the
one you love most. Sometimes a new life begins in tears."

XI. THE TRIAL

THE STORY of the Cross now moves forward to the scene before Pilate. Early in the morning, before the sun was up, the religious leaders turned Jesus over to the state. As a matter of fact, they had no authority to execute a man under the arrangements that then existed between Rome and the local government. I imagine that in this instance they were just as well pleased that they did not have such authority, for it relieved them of an embarrassing situation.

The church is often tempted to turn things over to the state. The church is likely to turn the whole matter of war over to the state. The church says, "We know it is wrong and against all Christian principles, so we turn it over to you. You manage it." The church is often content to turn criminals over to the state and say, "They have broken the law; we don't know what to do with them; so you do what you think ought to be done." Even more alarming is the fact that in recent years the church—I suppose not so much the church as society itself—is inclined to turn the family over to the state. Let the state make the divorce laws; let the state educate the children; let the state provide for the welfare of families when they are in trouble; let the state take care of people when they are too old to take care of themselves.

Pilate was in this case the representative of the state. He was Governor General of Judea for ten years, from A.D. 26 to 36. I wonder as I read the story again whether Pilate had any idea that he was living at the dawn of a new age. His position was similar to that of General MacArthur in Japan. He represented the government that was occupying the country. He must have been a fairly able man or he would not have been allowed to stay there for ten years. In one sense he was an ideal person to conduct the trial of Jesus because, unlike Caiaphas and the Sanhedrin, he had no prejudices about Jesus and no foregone conclusions; that is, he had an open mind to the whole question. But on the other hand, he had absolutely no knowledge of the case in hand.

Pilate, according to Mark's account, was at least direct. He asked Jesus, "Are you the King of the Jews?" How we wish we could catch the tone of voice in these conversations. It is wonderful to have them in print, but if we could only hear the tone of voice. Do you suppose when Pilate said that he said it almost with a sneer? "Are *you* the one they have been saying is King of the Jews, *you?*" Jesus was not quite so direct. He answered, "You say so." He did not say yes or no. I suppose the reason he resorted to indirection and evasion, if we may call it that, was the fact that he knew that what he meant and what Pilate meant by "King of the Jews" were two entirely different things. Pilate meant by "King of the Jews" someone who threatened to take over the Roman authority, and Jesus did not mean that at all. So it was hardly fair to use the same words.

And then, the story briefly and almost bluntly goes on to say that all this time the chief priests went on making additional charges against him. We wish we knew what these charges were but they are not indicated. I cannot help thinking as I read the story how amazing it is that no one stood up and said anything good about him. No one told what wonderful things he had done for the people in Galilee, how he had made sick people well and given people who were discouraged new hope. It seems as if someone in the group would have stood up and said, "Well, don't forget, he has done some wonderful things." But the chief priests went on making their charges and Jesus made no further reply.

The story goes on to say, "So Pilate wondered." You see the silence of Jesus is the framework of the whole picture. Pilate wondered! Of course he wondered. This was a different kind of prisoner from those he was used to dealing with, a man who made no pretense of defending himself, someone who did not even answer the charges. What kind of person was this? Pilate was not completely unimaginative or insensitive; he had the capacity to wonder. The trouble was he did not wonder deeply enough. Perhaps it would be more accurate if we said that he was curious but not greatly concerned, and there are many people like that. He saw through the motives of the high priests. He knew that they had brought Jesus there because they were jealous of him. He tried to get out of executing Jesus by resorting to a custom of releasing a prisoner on a festival and he suggested that he release Jesus to them. He said perfectly frankly, "I can't find that he is guilty of any of the things you say he is guilty of. He has done nothing that looks like treason."

But the crowd preferred another man by the name of Barabbas. I suppose in their language he might have been described as a "real man." He was a nationalist. He was patriotic. He was the kind of person who would stir a crowd. He liked to wave a flag and he was not afraid of being violent if necessary. A man like Jesus did not have a chance against a man like Barabbas. He would not today. The American public would do very much the same thing. You know what we are like when we get in a great throng. The average citizen would choose a patriotic American waving a flag, beating a drum, and making a great protest against Russia in preference to a man who stood up and said, "Blessed are the peacemakers for they shall be called the children of God."

So Pilate made his famous statement in the form of a question, "What then shall I do with Jesus?" And the people shouted, "Crucify him!" Pilate, the story goes on tragically to recount, "willing to content the people, or wishing to satisfy the crowd, released Barabbas unto them, and delivered Jesus, when he had scourged him, to be crucified."

Pilate, in a real sense, was to blame for the death of Jesus. After all, he was the governor of the land. He had the authority and he could have stopped it if he had wanted to. Why didn't he? Because he was not strong enough to resist the pressure of public opinion. He knew what was right but he did not dare to do it because he knew the people would not like it. And that is one of the dangers faced by everybody in any public office. It is a temptation even to a clergyman. There are times when he knows what is right but if he knows that the people would not like it, sometimes he does not dare to do it.

It is needless to point out how many men there are like that in public office today. And to come closer home, there are parents like that. They know what is right for their children but if the children do not like it, the parents are not always strong enough to do it. The weakness of these people is the same as Pilate's. He did not carry into his public life the moral insights of his private life. We often hear it said that some men are wonderful people in their offices but devils in their homes, or meek as lambs in their homes and devils when they get out into public life.

So it is written, "Jesus suffered under Pontius Pilate" and, in a way, Pilate bears the whole of the blame. And yet I think we have to say in fairness that Pilate was not alone to blame. After all, he was the representative of the Roman government and was carrying out its policies. It was partly to blame. Also, he was the product of a system, an imperial system, and that, too, was partly to blame. Furthermore, he was the front for local religious leaders and they carried a large part of the blame. He was also the tool of an angry mob. So the most we can say is that Pilate shared the blame with all these others. The blame for the Cross cannot be pinned on any one man. And when we get right down to it, the blame for anything can seldom be pinned on any one person. The blame for the war cannot be pinned on any one person. The blame for corruption in government cannot be pinned on any one person. And even the blame for the failure of a marriage cannot be pinned on any one party exclusively. As a matter of fact, Pilate was in something of a predicament. As a private citizen he had nothing against Jesus and he would have been perfectly willing to let him go. He did not care anything about him one way or the other. But as a public official he could not let him go. It was his job to keep the peace and to defend Roman rights, just as it was the job of the chief priest to defend the faith.

The situation in the world today is a predicament too great and complex for men to handle well. Nobody wants war but we have it. Do you ever feel that you yourself are in a predicament, that you are in a situation in which you cannot do exactly what you want to do? Too many factors are involved. You have too many commitments to children and friends, husband or wife, and job. Over and over again in trying to administer the affairs of a church, I feel that I am caught in a predicament and cannot do the thing I know is the right thing and the best thing. It is the predicament of our self-will and our human situation.

To go back to this scene before Pilate, the one person there who was not in a predicament was Jesus, the condemned man. He had no commitments to anybody but God. He had no loyalties to anything but the Kingdom of God. He had no customers, no clients, no constituents to satisfy. He could be himself, the king of a Kingdom not of this world. And as he stood there before Pilate, who represented the power and authority of the kingdoms of this world, Jesus asserted his claim silently and quietly to be the king forever of that invisible and eternal realm. No wonder people ever since have turned to him in their predicaments. If he cannot do anything else for us he can take the curse off our predicament.

XII. THE CRUCIFIXION

WE NOW move on in the story of the Cross to the Crucifixion itself. Crucifixion was the Roman method ef execution. It was for slaves, not citizens. The Jews preferred stoning. Both were cruel and brutal forms of torture.

We do not want to dwell unduly on the physical side of the Crucifixion, but neither do we want to by-pass it altogether and forget the pain and physical suffering. A crucifixion proceeded as follows. The arms of a man were bound on a crossbar (sometimes they were nailed but more likely bound) which he himself had carried to the place of execution, and then it was lifted up and fastened to a permanent post in the ground. Death was by exposure and starvation.

We stop for a minute to think how cruel human beings can be to one another. There is something in us that makes us want to hurt people deliberately, and we cannot escape that fact by saying that it is part of our public responsibility to punish people who have done wrong. The concentration camps in Germany, of course, are illustrations of the cruelty of men, but I think we ought to be much more concerned with our own homes. I have known grown children to do things deliberately to hurt their parents, and I have known parents who do things deliberately to hurt their children. And of course we have all known people in places of authority who have done things to hurt people who work under them, to make them squirm. This is a time when we ought to acknowledge how cruel human beings can be.

They crucified Jesus on a low hill, apparently outside the city wall. As it was a hill that looked something like a skull, it was called Golgotha. It has long since been erased by the ravages of time and there is no use in trying to determine exactly where it was. They began the procedure at nine o'clock in the morning on what was probably a very hot day. The passers-by were interested in what was going on. They were used to such sights. Some of them sneered at him and said, "Save yourself. You claim to be able to do all sorts of wonderful things, now prove it." The chief priests joked among themselves and said, "He saved others; himself he cannot save." And the two who were crucified with him reviled him.

The physical pain was bad enough, and though it has been our custom in recent years not to dwell on physical pain, nevertheless, it is real and people who suffer know what it is. But this was much worse than physical pain. The derision of the people must have been even more difficult to bear. I wonder if Jesus had ever been made fun of as a little boy because he liked to go to the synagogue when other boys may have been playing ball. The experience of having our words twisted so that they mean something entirely different is one of the hardest things we face.

To make matters even worse, not one of Jesus' friends was there. There were some women watching from a distance what went on. People are always quick to point out the fact that there are always more women in church than there are men. It is deplorable and a judgment on the men, but that must not blind us to the fact that women have been largely responsible for carrying as in a vessel some of the most precious things of life.

Years later, when John wrote his Gospel, he apparently could not bear the fact that there was not at least one friend there, and he wrote into his story that Jesus' mother and his best friend, John, were there. Maybe they were; I hope they were. But it does not seem likely, since neither Mark nor Matthew nor Luke mentions it.

What did Jesus say while all this was going on? Tradition has it that he spoke seven times. Let us look impartially and objectively at the words. Three of them are in Luke's Gospel and in none of the others. "Father forgive them for they know not what they do." "Today shalt thou be with me in paradise." "Father, into thy hands I commend my spirit." Three of them are in John's Gospel only. "Woman, behold thy son." "I thirst." "It is finished." And in Matthew and Mark there is only one word and it is not a word at all, it is a loud cry: "My God, my God, why hast thou forsaken me?" Some people are sure this last was a shout of triumph because it is the first line of one of the great Messianic psalms. Some people are equally sure that it was a human cry of desolation. We do not know which it was. All the words that Luke and John have attributed to him on the Cross are in character. They are words we know he would be likely to say. Two of them were prayers: "Father, forgive them"; "Father, into thy hands I commend my spirit." Two were considerations for other people, the penitent thief and his mother; and two were brief references to himself—his thirst and his death.

But this cry that is in the earliest tradition of Mark and Matthew is the one, I think, that makes the deepest impression on the people of our time. It is the one, certainly, that brings Jesus closer to us. How often we feel that not only have our friends deserted us and life has gone back on us but that even God is far away and remote, and does not seem to care one way or the other. It helps me to think that Jesus in his hour had the same experience, as though the heavens were falling in upon him. It did not last, it never lasts, thank God, but while we feel that way, life can be very dark.

More important, of course, than what he said is what he did. Every year in Holy Week I get out a little book by Richard Roberts, the Canadian preacher, called *That Strange Man on the Cross*. Hundreds of books have been written about the Cross but for some reason there is no other book that reaches me the way this one does. One of the lines that I underlined the first time I read it and that I always go back to is this: "On Calvary, Jesus said little and did nothing." He had had his say and he had done all that needed to be done. For one thing he did none of the things that most people would have tried to do. He did not try to get away. He did not call on divine resources even though he may have felt that legions of angels were at his command. He did not try to defend himself. He did not argue with his accusers. He did not try to get back at them. He did not even get angry with them. He did not try to hurt anybody. He gave no sign that he was bitter or regretful, and in that sense, to be sure, he did nothing. If we only had the grace to know when to take things.

Jesus was not always like that. He did not always let people make away with him. When they threatened to destroy his life up in Galilee, he was very shrewd and took steps to save himself and to get away. But he knew this was the time when the thing for him to do was to take it and by his attitude to show people forever how to take the things that must be taken.

Yet, in another sense, he never did more than he did on Calvary. It was as though for the first time he rose to his full height. If we could only get even an imperfect glimpse of what he was like. He did not, you see, resign himself to the Cross. He took it up. He went out to meet it.

In the garden, after he had fought it out with himself and with God and had determined to do the will of God, he saw Judas and the temple police coming toward him. He said, "Arise, let us be going." In other words, he seemed to feel that this was his great chance to show the people what he meant by love. You can talk about something like love from now until doomsday, but people will never know what you mean until you practice it. So many times in sermons I try to define Christian love and I suppose it is worth doing, but it is not the definition of love that counts. It is the demonstration of it. To go out and forgive the unforgivable and love the unlovable means more than all the definitions and understandings of love that you or I or anybody else will ever entertain.

It is almost impossible for us to believe that Jesus could have loved those people. I do not believe that we should have loved them, even at our best. I have known a few people who have had an amazing capacity to love, but I am not so sure about myself. Could I love those people if they had me on the spot? I do not believe I could. Could you?

That is the reason, you see, why people have felt that in Jesus the love of God came near. Such love is not in man except as he reveals the love of God. Only God could love like that. A Jewish rabbi by the name of Johannan once wrote this: "The ministering angels wanted to sing a hymn at the destruction of the Egyptians." You remember all the pictures that those words suggest: the Jews were finally led out of slavery, the Egyptians were killed, and the Jews were free. Quite naturally, the ministering angels wanted to sing a hymn. But God said, "My children lie drowned in the sea and you would sing?" The Egyptians were his children, too.

Pilate and the chief priests, the soldiers and the crowd, the deserting disciples—they were all God's children and could the Son of God be bitter toward them? You see it takes a love like that to cleanse us from our sins. Nothing less can do it. Anything more is beyond our imagination. And in a way there is nothing more to say about the Cross. It is the story of the love that will not let us go. We listen to it year in and year out and we find that each year the love becomes more amazing, more divine.

XIII.   THE BURIAL

We now bring the story of the Cross to a close. We have passed the climax and we come to a quiet conclusion.

Jesus died in six hours; we are told that it usually took twelve for a crucified man to die. We do not know why Jesus died more quickly than other people; it may have been that he was not quite so robust. We do not really know what he was like physically, except by implication. In recent years we have tried to make him into a modern, sun-burned, athletic American youth who could endure all the physical hardships of life. He may not have been like that at all. He may have been a sensitive, delicate, rather frail person, physically speaking.

It was a law of the Jews that a body could not remain on the cross overnight because it would pollute the Holy Land. The question was, Who would come to take Jesus' body away? Of course, we should have assumed that his family would take his body, or his friends; but they did not. Where they were we do not know, but no friend appeared and nobody in the family turned up; a man who emerged from the shadows of obscurity took the body—Joseph of Arimathea. (Arimathea, another of those words, like Gethsemane, that haunts you with the beauty of its sound.)

The record says quite simply that he took courage and went to Pilate and asked for the body of Jesus. It did take courage because he was a rich man and apparently a prominent man, and had some official position in the town of Arimathea, where he came from. He may have been on the local Sanhedrin there, and it took courage for him to go to the head of the government and indicate his sympathy with Jesus and with what he represented. Of course, we cannot help but wish that Joseph had had a little courage earlier in the day; we cannot help but wish that, when all the high priests were bringing charges against Jesus, this man from Arimathea had stood up and told them some of the wonderful things Jesus had done. But he did not. There are a great many people who do not have the courage when we should like to have them have it. But nevertheless Joseph of Arimathea came to the point where he risked the dangers involved and asked Pilate for the body of Jesus.

Then notice how carefully he treated it. He wrapped the body in a fine linen shroud and laid it in a tomb hewn out of rock. It was a tomb he had had made for himself, and nobody had ever lain in it before; when he put Jesus in it he knew that no one else ever could use it because it was against the law for any other free Jew to be buried in the same grave with a criminal. So it was the end of the tomb for Joseph. And then he rolled a great stone against the door to seal it.

In the midst of so much hardness and cruelty, here is the tenderness of Joseph of Arimathea. Wherever you go you will find it. I have never had the privilege of serving in the armed forces, but I have known many men who have and they all tell the same story, that no matter how brutal the scene, and no matter how charged it is with violence, there are always people who are ready to minister to the men who are dying, always stretcher-bearers and nurses, always somebody who is tender in the midst of all that hardness. It is easy for us to grow bitter and cynical about human beings, and it is a great tragedy when we do. We certainly do not want to be unduly optimistic about them or under any illusions about their weaknesses. We want to see the facts as they are. But when we begin to think that everybody is hard-hearted and nobody has any interest in other people, we can remember Joseph of Arimathea, who out of his security and safety had the courage to go and ask Pilate if he could have the body of Jesus.

It was more than tenderness, really; it was respect for the human body. There are religions that despise the body; they talk about it as the prison-house of the soul and say that the sooner we get out of it the better. Christianity has never been like that. Christianity has always respected and reverenced the body, partly because when God wanted to come among us he took a body in which to dwell. God manifest himself in a body, and it is certainly to the credit of the race that this body of Jesus, wracked with pain and deprived now of life, was not carelessly cast aside. We are grateful to Joseph for that. And beyond that, there was reverence for the dignity of an individual. Here was the body of a dead man that had once been aglow with life. Though limp and lifeless now, he was once a real person, and no one else will ever be exactly like him. He was an unmatchable individual.

This burial was all anybody could do at the time; the deed had been done and it could not be undone. There was nothing anyone could do to bring Jesus back to life, and most people, I am afraid, would have said, "There is nothing to do, nothing can be done now, let's go home." Joseph said, "There isn't anything to do except to bury the body, and to treat it with the care and the reverence that every human body deserves." It was the only thing to be done at the time, and the right thing to be done, and Joseph did it.

What I want to stress most is that the Cross drew the best out of Joseph. We know very little about Joseph; we can only speculate and imagine what he was like, but it is fair to suppose that the tenderness of this man was a response to the gallantry of Jesus. Something that might have been forever dormant in him was drawn out of him by the Cross. And the Cross has been doing that ever since. It draws out of rather ordinary, average human individuals such as we, things that are greater than we dreamed possible. Edwin Arlington Robinson has a poem describing a poet, and I think you will see how it applies to the situation we are concerned with.

> To get at the eternal strength of things,
> And fearlessly to make strong songs of it
> Is, in my mind, the mission of that man
> The world would call a poet. He may sing
> But roughly and withal ungraciously;
> But if he touch to life the one right chord
> Wherein God's music slumbers, and awake
> To truth one drowsed ambition, he sings well.

Because Jesus somehow touched to life the one right chord wherein God's music slumbers, and by his Cross awakes to truth our drowsed ambition, some of us will be more tender when we go out of our homes today than we were when we came in.

Even if this were the last chapter in the story, even if the tomb were the end and the stone were rolled against the door of it with a finality that nothing could ever disturb, the Cross would still be the chief glory of the human race. The Cross was originally a tree growing somewhere on one of the hillsides of Palestine, a good, beautiful, natural thing. Men took it and cut it down and twisted it into an instrument of torture, and Jesus turned it into a throne of glory. And even if there had been no Resurrection, men would never have forgotten it. It was the way Jesus met humiliation, pain, misunderstanding, violence, the way he met the Cross, the way he bore his Cross, that makes all our crosses easier to bear.

It is hard to put into words what the Cross of Christ means to us. Sometimes I find in expressions that have nothing directly to do with the Cross reflections that illuminate the Cross for me. One of these is a poem by Robert Frost:

> *Oh, stormy, stormy world,*
> *The days you were not swirled*
> *Around with mist and cloud,*
> *Or wrapped as in a shroud,*
> *And the sun's brilliant ball*
> *Was not in part or all*
> *Obscured from mortal view—*

Were days so very few
I can but wonder whence
I get the lasting sense
Of so much warmth and light.
If my mistrust is right
It may be altogether
From one day's perfect weather,
When starting clear at dawn,
The day swept clearly on
To finish clear at eve.
I verily believe
My fair impression may
Be all from that one day
No shadow crossed but ours
As through its blazing flowers
We went from house to wood
For change of solitude.*

We live in a stormy world. There is so much pain and so much unfairness and so much injustice, so many people bearing handicaps that they do not seem to have deserved at all, that I sometimes wonder how I get that lasting sense of warmth and light and love. It may be altogether from one day's perfect weather, when one man met life perfectly.

We cannot get away from the stone over the door of the sepulchre. It looks like the end of the story, and as the evangelists record, Mary Magdalene and Mary, the mother of Joseph, saw where he was laid. How their hearts must

---

have sunk when they saw the stone rolled against the door. Oh, deceiving stone. As we look at the gravestone, may the Lord give us the power to see through the stones of life to the future that lies ahead. This story of the Cross is full of irony, but never is the irony so marked as it is at this point. We know what the next chapter is, and yet there is the stone. We must never let the stones of life stop us.

XIV. THE RESURRECTION

As THE story of Jesus began in mystery, it ended in mystery that words are powerless to describe. Some of us would give almost anything to know exactly what happened on the first Easter Day, not merely for the sake of idle curiosity, and not only because we should like to know what will happen to us when we die (and if we knew what happened to Jesus when *he* died that might throw light on our own death) but because we sincerely want to know what happened to *him*. We want to know how the story of Jesus came out. What happened to the idea of the Kingdom that he had, which he talked about so much, and promised the people so confidently? What happened to the life he was so eager to communicate to people? Was it all snuffed out like a candle at the end? Did the universe turn thumbs down on Jesus? Like every child who listens to a story, we want to know how it all came out. We want to know what happened to him. We want to know if it is really true that he who came to tell people about a Kingdom, and to show people what that Kingdom of life was like, ended his life on a Cross, defeated, rejected by the world, and plowed into oblivion by the quiet passing of the years.

I

The probability is that we shall never know exactly what happened on the first Easter Day. The events were reported by a great many people, and they were ultimately written down by five or six people. Those people made their report, as you might expect, according to their own observations, which were not all alike, and according to their own understanding and their own interpretation of what happened. Moreover, they all made their report under the influence of the spell—you might say of the rapture—into which the event rocketed them. They wrote not in a spirit of calm and disinterested objectivity but in a state of excitement. No wonder their reports do not always agree; in fact, sometimes they are flatly contradictory. We are not surprised by this any more than we are if five men reporting what happened on D-Day do not all report exactly the same thing. So, we begin by acknowledging the fact that we shall never know exactly what happened on Easter Day.

There are, however, some things that we do know for certain, and it will help us to set down in black and white; they will give us a standing-place from which to reach for the things that are far beyond us.

We know, in the first place, that Jesus appeared to his friends after he died. He did not appear, according to any record, to the general public; he did not suddenly turn up in the courts of the temple, or in Pilate's palace, or in the middle of a crowd. Apparently, the people in general never saw him after Good Friday the way they saw him when he appeared on Palm Sunday. No, he appeared to his friends, to the ones who wanted to see him, who were prepared to see him, who longed to see him and were glad when they did see him.

And he appeared first, the record says, to Peter, just as we might expect; the one who was closest to him, in greatest sympathy with him. Then he appeared to all the other disciples; and then to quite a large group of friends, five hundred, the account says; and then to the women who had followed him faithfully to the Cross, the only ones of his friends who were there; then, last of all, and several months after the Resurrection, to Paul, the Apostle, who spoke of his own vision of Christ on the Damascus Road in the same terms in which he spoke of the Resurrection appearances Jesus made to the others.

As far as I can see, there would have been no reason for their saying that Jesus appeared to them if he had not. And there certainly would not have been any reason for their risking their lives for it and dying for it if they knew it was a lie. So, if we put any confidence in the people who reported the story of Jesus, it is hard to see how we can escape the fact, incredible as it may seem to us, that Jesus appeared to some of them after he died. That is the first thing we know.

We also know that in most cases it was not a physical appearance—at least it gives no sign of being a physical appearance. He came and went through closed doors, and physical bodies as we know them do not do that. He walked on the water; he appeared simultaneously in Jerusalem and in Galilee. He was not always recognized by his friends when he appeared, as you would expect him to be if he were the same body that they had been familiar with in the days of his earthly life. Not only was he not recognized but some even doubted that they had seen him at all. (The accounts are exceedingly honest in regard to these matters.) He appeared to Paul as a glorified figure in the sky. So we can put down as one of the certainties about the Resurrection of Jesus that whatever the appearances he made to his friends were like, they were not purely and simply physical appearances.

And yet the appearances were so real that stories, such as the story of Thomas thrusting his hand into Jesus' side, could be very freely circulated, and the story of the empty tomb could finally become the most beloved of them all. In other words, what the reporters were trying to say was this: "The appearance of Jesus was to us more than a glorified memory; it was that to be sure, for we do have wonderful memories of what he said and what he did, but this was more than a memory, however much glorified. And it was different from an hallucination, because normally two people do not have the same hallucination at the same time. We really saw something. It was a real appearance. It was vivid enough to convince rather unimaginative and stupid people that Jesus was alive, and that God ruled as Jesus said he did."

That much we can put down for certain—that Jesus appeared to his friends, that the appearances, though not physical, convinced his friends that he was alive. Preaching in the city of Antioch several years later, Paul was sketching the history of his people Israel, how they had been chosen by God for a special purpose in the world. When he came to the story of Jesus, he told them how he was born, how John the Baptist had prepared the way for him, how he went about doing good, and how he was condemned and put to death; then Paul went on to say, "They took him down from the Cross and laid him in a tomb; but God raised him from the dead, and during the course of many days he appeared to those who had come up with him from Galilee to Jerusalem." That is the New Testament story of the Resurrection in a nutshell. So much for the records.

II

We are not antiquarians or historians. Our interest in this matter is from the point of view of our own lives and the problems we have to deal with, and the temperaments and dispositions we have to make the most of in life. What we gather from all this is that death was by no means the end of Jesus. We do not pretend to say that Jesus is present with us as our friends are present; what we do say is that he is present as spirit and power and truth, and that when we read the story of Jesus, the figure of Jesus is alive, not dead. He speaks to us not from the grave but as a real and contemporary Person. We know him and feel his presence among us. Furthermore, we say that if Jesus is alive, the things he lived and died for are real and true.

The fact that Jesus is alive means that God really does rule the world; that God really does rule your life. It means that God really does care for you as an individual.

It means that the hairs of your head are all numbered; it means that the gentle shall inherit the earth in spite of all the evidences to the contrary; it means that love really is the only key that can unlock the gates of life; it means that those who humble themselves really will be exalted. It means that he that loseth his life will really find it; it means that if a grain of wheat is cast into the ground and left to die, it will bear much fruit; it means that God really did so love the world that he gave his only begotten Son that whosoever believeth in him shall not perish but have everlasting life.

It means that death was not the end of him, and that all the things that were represented by him and incarnate in him exist and are true and present among us now. It means that beyond this realm of time and space and physical circumstance, of life and disease and disaster and tragedy, there is a realm without boundary where things of the spirit reign, and where individuals continue to pursue their lives in the presence of their Maker even though we cannot see them. All these things the Resurrection of Jesus means. These mighty facts are not bubbles that were pricked by the sword-point of death. They are realities that all the forces of evil could not overthrow.

And so we come to the end of our story of Jesus. And yet it is not the end, because as the story began with God, so it ends with God, and God has no beginning or ending. When we talked about the birth of Jesus we said that the important thing was that Jesus came from God, and on Easter we profess the faith that he went to God. The Resurrection is not so much the story of how Jesus returned to the earth as it is the story of how this life that once came among us returned to heaven, to the presence of God, the realm of the eternal and infinite, where he now reigns as the Young Prince of Glory.

It makes all the difference in the world to me to know and believe that Jesus is alive, and that the Kingdom of God for which he gave his life is alive and powerful and true and real; and it means that the only way you or I will ever find our lives is by way of that Kingdom, by way of that Cross, and by the price of that love. There is no other way, and that is why our hearts are filled with gratitude on Easter Day as we try to put into words what is really beyond the range of words: that Jesus, though not in a physical presence, though not visible, though not here among us now as one we can see, nevertheless lives and reigns forever, and that his spirit can be in us and that we can be in him.

> *I know not how that Bethlehem's babe*
> *Could in the Godhead be;*
> *I only know the manger child*
> *Has brought God's life to me.*
>
> *I know not how that Calvary's cross*
> *A world from sin could free;*
> *I only know its matchless love*
> *Has brought God's love to me.*
>
> *I know not how that Joseph's tomb*
> *Could solve death's mystery;*
> *I only know a living Christ,*
> *Our immortality.* [*]

---

[*] Reprinted by permission of the Hymn Society of America.

XV. THE CHURCH

THE STORY of the church began when the individual followers of Jesus became a *body* in which his spirit could
live and continue its work in the world. The day on which
that happened we call Pentecost. We call it that for the
simple reason that it happened on the Jewish festival called
Pentecost, the day the Jews celebrated the giving of the
law, roughly fifty days after the Passover. Exactly what
happened on that day we do not know; it is never easy
for people who go through great experiences to describe
them in words, and the people who went through this experience found it especially difficult to describe. They used
such figures of speech as "a rushing mighty wind" and
"flames of fire." They tried as best they could to say that
they were suddenly possessed by a great power, that something took hold of them, that they were enabled to do great
things far beyond their natural capacities.

We all know surely that there is a difference between
individuals acting separately and a body of men. It is one
thing to see a group of individual musicians, each playing
his own instrument in his own way, and quite another

thing to see a group of musicians become a body of musicians, which in turn becomes the instrument upon which a composer or a conductor can perform the masterworks of music. The individual loses his identity in the larger body, and yet finds his own fulfillment as a member of that body. Something like that happened on Pentecost; a group of individuals became a body which the spirit of Jesus could use to continue his work in the world.

I

Lets us look a little more carefully at the beginning of the church. There was, at least it seems to me, very little conscious planning on the part of Jesus. There is no evidence in the New Testament to lead us to believe that Jesus ever attempted to design a great institution. He never baptized anybody; he never ordained anybody; in fact, as far as we know, he never used the word "church" at all. He himself remained all his life within the pale of the religious community of Judaism. He left no organization behind him except, in the word of Baron von Hugel, the Roman Catholic theologian, "his modest organization of the little preaching and curing fraternity of his Apostles." Jesus left a handful of picked men that he had kept close to him and trained in the principles of the Kingdom. Other than that he left no organization, no institution.

What about the verse in Matthew in which Jesus says to Peter, "Thou art Peter, and upon this rock will I build my church"? That is a controversial text, to say the least, over which too much blood has already been spilled. This is not the place to prolong the controversy or to inquire into its pros and cons. All we can say here is that if Jesus said it, it is hardly conceivable that he meant to establish anything like that hierarchy of power and monarchical line of bishops which a large part of Christendom thinks he meant to establish. Even though he recognized Peter's natural gift for leadership, it is impossible for some of us to believe that Jesus meant to fix the pattern of the future in a mold that could be neither changed nor criticized. It is much more likely that he never said the words. In the same passage as recorded by Mark, which is the earlier account, that word to Peter is not included, and good authorities on the New Testament now tell us that it is much more likely that the line was added later to suit the condition that existed at the end of the first century, in a community in Palestine where Peter and his successors had already taken a place of leadership.

We must leave this complicated question with those few words, emphasizing the fact that in the course of Jesus' lifetime he did very little, if anything, to plan for an elaborate institution called the Church.

Rather, the church grew spontaneously, naturally, as the followers of Jesus responded to new and changing circumstances in an effort to meet the needs of a world that was constantly changing, and in which they tried to do the best they could to act in the name of Jesus. It grew, of course, among the people who remembered Jesus; somehow they could not get that Figure out of their minds. They did not always understand him, they were not always loyal to him, by any means, but they could not forget him, and the church as we know it began as "the fellowship of those people who remembered Jesus" and who could not betray that memory.

It is worth remembering, too, that the church began among the lower classes, among the peasants, the poor, the artisans, the laborers, the slaves; people who had nothing in life, who felt they had been more or less forgotten by man and God. They were the people who were ripe for the message that not only did God rule but that he cared—that God cared for them and for everything that concerned ᵗʰ ᵐ, and that times would be better. It was these people, who had little or nothing, who responded to the message first, and among whom the church spread like wildfire.

For a long time it was an underground movement. The Jews did not like it any more than we should like it today if a group of people left the church and began a little movement on the side, by themselves. The Jews looked on Christians as disloyal members of Judaism, and they scorned them. Rome persecuted them, so that for two or three hundred years this movement had to keep hidden, meeting in places where it would not be discovered. Many of the great movements of the world have begun as underground movements. So the church began not so much by planning as by the spontaneous response of the people who remembered and loved Jesus to the spirit of Jesus as they felt it alive among them.

II

From such a beginning the church grew by leaps and bounds. It soon began to attract, as movements of this kind usually do, the intellectuals; Paul was one of the first, then Origen, Iranaeus, Augustine, and the great Tertullian. There were others here and there who had the wits to see in this underground movement among the lower classes in society the light of the future of the world. And they set themselves to perform one of the tasks that always has to be performed in any movement such as this, at some point in its history—that of interpreting the meaning of what had been happening in terms of the science and philosophy of their day. Because we are thinking creatures we cannot be content merely to do things. We must have some understanding of what we do. We are bound to make some attempt to fit what we do and what happens to us into the total scheme of life as we understand it. And so these intellectuals, one here and another there, in these first centuries, set themselves to the task of interpreting the meaning of this movement in terms of the philosophy and science of the time. The Apostles' Creed and the Nicene Creed are the chief monuments of their efforts.

Finally, the time came when this underground movement came up on the surface, out into the light. It was recognized by men of power to be a movement with great force in it. Some of the rulers were converted to it, and Christianity gradually became what we call an established religion. No more persecuted, it was put in a place of prominence; it made that dangerous move from the Upper Room to the courts and palaces of rulers, from paupers to princes, from rags to riches. It began to have power, to accumulate wealth, to have all the protection it needed, and to attract great numbers of people. A converted king baptized his army en masse as he forded a river. In fact, the

time came when the church and the state became coterminous, so to speak. The church was no longer a minority
group within the state; the church and the state were two
sides of the same thing. When people spoke about art,
they were speaking about Christian art, because there was
no other art. When they spoke about education, they spoke
about Christian education because there was no other education. When they deliberated in the governments of the
world, they were deliberating in Christian governments,
because there were no other governments. And, tragic
though it may be, when they fought their wars, they fought
religious wars, because there were no other wars. The
church gained in power, in wealth, and in influence. That
cannot be denied. *Instead of being the leaven in the lump,
it became the lump.*

III

The church in our time is in a still different position, not
actually persecuted as it was in the beginning, or powerful
as it was in the Middle Ages. The church is now once more
disestablished, in fact if not in theory. In England, to be
sure, it is established, but only in theory, for in fact the
Church and the government are as far apart as the poles
when it comes to the sharing of authority or the formulat-
ing of policy. In this country, the church never has been
established; it is not only not tied up with the state, it is
nowhere near coterminous with our civilization. Our art
is anything but Christian art, our education is only tinged
with Christianity, our politics have little or no concern with

Christian ethics, and our business pays only formal respect to them.

Science, I suppose, has done more than anything else to dethrone the church from its former place of prestige. Its theories and its dogmas and its teachings have been seriously questioned, and some of the secondary ones have been discredited, so that the church in our time is once more on the defensive, in the minority, and maybe, before we are through, it will be back in the catacombs again. The question is, of course, can the church rise again? Can the church, which has fallen from the peak of power that it reached in the Middle Ages, ever rise to anything like that place again?

I, for one, am sure that it will rise, though perhaps in not exactly the same form, and I am one of those who will not insist that the form be the same. The form might well be improved, adapted to new conditions and circumstances. No machinery lasts forever, and from time to time it needs not only to be repaired but occasionally to be replaced. But Christ's spirit is alive in the world, there is no doubt about that. The giving, the compassion, the redeeming love are just as much alive today as they were in the Middle Ages, or in the first century. And if the church as it is cannot provide a body for Christ's spirit, it will find one somewhere else. But it will not be defeated, it will find an agent, an instrument somewhere in the world to carry out its work of reclaiming men's lives. I am sure that in that sense the church will rise again.

There are just three brief comments that I should like to make as a conclusion to this story. The first is that the best results are not always produced by the best planning. Jesus apparently did not plan a great institution for an unknown future; he produced men who were trained to do the will of God each day. We must plan, and we must plan for the future of the church, but if the church is ever to rise again, it will be not by our elaborate planning but by our willingness to respond to the will of God in whatever situation we happen to find ourselves. Flexibility, not rigidity, is the key.

The second comment is that most great movements begin among the lower classes. The upper classes are likely to be softened by their wealth and hardened by their power, and if there is to be a revival of the church in our time, it is almost certain that it will be among those people who are on the lower shelves of society, the psychologically lost, the people who feel that there is no purpose or point in the world and who are trying to find their way through the labyrinth of despair and doubt, the people who have been left out and passed over.

And the last comment is this: the church is often most influential when it is least powerful. I cannot be sure of this, but I should venture to say that the church is more influential today in India and China, where it is least powerful, than it is anywhere else in the world. I think that the clue for us is to think once more of the *leaven* in the lump, and to let the lump go, at least for the time being. If we can produce in our churches small groups of men and women who, remembering Jesus, are willing to do everything in their power to be of use to him, to bring compassion in place of compulsion, to make every sacrifice, and to go into their family and business situations as the reconciling agents of the Son of God, then we shall become once again the leaven in the lump, and the church will become the body of Christ, a living body, responsive to his needs and to his demands.